God, Girls, and Getting Connected

Robin Marsh
Lauren Nelson

HARVEST HOUSE PUBLISHERS

EUGENE, OREGON

Robin Marsh and Lauren Nelson are represented by Working Title Agency, LLC, Spring Hill, TN.

Backcover authors photo by gfellerstudio.com

Cover by Dugan Design Group, Bloomington, Minnesota

Cover photo © Tara Flake / Shutterstock

GOD, GIRLS, AND GETTING CONNECTED
Copyright © 2012 by Robin Marsh and Lauren Nelson
Published by Harvest House Publishers
Eugene, Oregon 97402
www.harvesthousepublishers.com

Library of Congress Cataloging-in-Publication Data
Marsh, Robin.
God, girls, and getting connected / Robin Marsh and Lauren Nelson.
p. cm.
ISBN 978-0-7369-4521-9 (pbk.)
ISBN 978-0-7369-4522-6 (eBook)
1. Teenage girls—Prayers and devotions. 2. Christian teenagers—Prayers and devotions. I. Nelson, Lauren. II. Title.
BV4860.M36 2012
248.8'33—dc23
                                        2011021177

Printed in the United States of America

12 13 14 15 16 17 18 19 20 / BP-SK / 10 9 8 7 6 5 4 3 2

● ●

To Dr. Alan Day

1948–2011

Pastor. Teacher. Friend.

● ●

Acknowledgments

Keith, you are a wonderful husband and godly man. Words can never express how much I love you. Your unconditional love and support never waver.

Cade, you are a terrific son. My prayer is that when you grow up and find a special woman to marry, she will be connected to God in every area of her life.

Love,
Robin

Randy, God blessed me beyond what I deserve when He brought you into my life to be my husband. You are always such a wonderful source of support, wisdom, and encouragement. Without you I wouldn't be where I am today. Thank you for modeling Jesus to me every day. I love you!

Love,
Lauren

Many more people helped make this project happen—too many to mention by name. But there are a few we'd like to especially thank.

Bill Reeves, our literary agent: We are grateful for your guidance and willingness to help.

The great people at Harvest House—especially Bob Hawkins, LaRae Weikert, and Hope Lyda: Thanks for believing in our vision to see teen girls' lives changed by knowing God.

Dr. Alan Day, Dr. Michael Catt, Dr. Anthony Jordan, and Dr. Ted Kersh: As godly pastors you help us see the life-changing power in the Word of God and encourage us to tell others about the saving grace of the Lord. Thank you.

Jesus, our Lord: Thank You for the relationships You blessed us with to bring this project to life and glorify Your name. We love You.

Contributing Consultant

Kelly King is the women's missions and ministries specialist for the Baptist General Convention of Oklahoma. She has worked with teen girls in her church for more than 20 years. In addition to teaching teens, she's written student discipleship materials for several publishers, including LifeWay Christian Resources and Student Life Publishing.

Contributing Writers

Natalee Hitchcock's enthusiasm for Christ is contagious. She majored in public relations at Oklahoma State University while serving as a cheerleader and in various leadership roles at Pi Beta Phi sorority. Natalee and her husband, Justin, are newlyweds and spend their time teaching and serving the youth at their church.

Christy Johnson, a dynamic speaker and author of *Rehab for Love Junkies, The 7 Must Haves for Soul-healthy Women,* is passionate about teaching young women how to develop essential habits that are foundational for healthy romantic relationships. Visit her at www.christyjohnson.org.

Mindy Mizell serves as media relations director for World Vision, a Christian humanitarian organization dedicated to working with children, families, and their communities worldwide to reach their full potential by tackling the causes of poverty and injustice. She deploys internationally for breaking news and emergency responses. Mindy's media experience includes freelancing for Fox, CBS, NBC, and ABC. She enjoys working with youth.

Kelsey Nail is a full-time college student majoring in Bible with a minor in theater. Her dream is to use her gifts and talents in the arts to communicate God's message of love and hope. In addition, she enjoys mentoring younger girls and serving in various areas at their church.

Lisa Nail has spent many years in full-time ministry as a pastor's wife, teaching women's Bible studies, and counseling women. She and her husband have been married 29 years and have two children. Lisa and her husband currently serve in several areas of ministry at their church.

Sherry Roberts, the mother of four, is a talented interior designer with a passion for living life to the fullest. She's spent the last 20-plus years telling friends and anyone who will listen about the love of Jesus Christ. Sherry is a Bible Study Fellowship leader. Sherry and her husband, Jerry, serve in various areas of ministry and counseling.

Staci Wekenborg has followed Christ since 1993. Her family has been involved in planting some of the fastest-growing churches in America. She is a leader, teacher, and servant for young girls and women in her community. This is her first time as a contributing writer and proof that God uses the ordinary to do His extraordinary work.

*You are incredible girlfriends, and we are indebted to you for
your prayers, your ideas, and your part in creating this devotional.
This has definitely been a team effort.
We love you more than you will ever know.*

Keith & Robin

Lauren, Tiffany, Sherry, Robin, Natalee

Occupation: Television news anchor/reporter (25+ years)

Employer: KWTV News9—CBS, Oklahoma City, OK

Relationship Status: Married to Keith

Children: Son, Cade, 11 years (He has the bluest eyes you'll ever see!)

Favorite Quote: "When you get to the end of your rope...tie a knot and hang on."—Franklin Roosevelt

Favorite Scripture: Ephesians 5 is my life passage. The first verse is "Follow God's example, therefore, as dearly loved children and walk in the way of love."

Favorite Interviews for Television: Garth Brooks, Reba McEntire (both Okies)

Toughest Day Ever to Be on Live TV: April 19, 1995: When the Alfred P. Murrah Federal building in Oklahoma City was bombed and 168 people lost their lives.

Favorite Book: The Bible and *Just Like Jesus* by Max Lucado

Most Embarrassing Moment: When a greeter at Walmart asked, "Are you Robin Marsh, the news lady on channel 9?" I said, "Yep, that's me." She then said, "You look better on TV!" (How humbling!)

Favorite Food: Italian...it comes naturally. My mom is Italian.

Pet Peeve: When people lose their gratefulness.

Activities: I enjoy reading, exercising, and speaking at ministry retreats for women and teen girls. My family means everything to me, and there's never a dull moment when my mom and sister are around! I love being mom to an awesome young man. I like to laugh. I'm always plotting ways to surprise people. *One time for a friend's birthday I schemed to have her come through the drive-thru at a fast-food restaurant. She didn't know it, but I was the one taking her order, and I kept messing it up. She was not a happy customer. You can imagine her face when she came to the window and saw me handing over her food! What fun!*

Cade & Robin

Day I Met Jesus: I grew up knowing about Jesus but had a life-changing experience at a church service in Amarillo, Texas. The preacher shared how Christ died on the cross for me so I could have eternal life. God was knocking on my heart's door, and I knew I could no longer ignore the call to be completely sold-out to Him. It remains the best decision I've ever made.

What Lauren Says About Robin: Robin is the most genuine person I know. What you see is what you get. I love that about her!

Lauren Nelson (Miss America, 2007)

Lauren & Morgan   Robin & Lauren

Occupation: Television news anchor, worship leader

Employer: KWTV News9—CBS, Oklahoma City, OK; First Baptist Church, Edmond, OK

Relationship Status: Married to Randy

Children: None today...but someday

Favorite Quote: "One of the most important parts of fulfilling your destiny is transparency. Our destiny is not just for ourselves but for others."—Beth Moore

Favorite Scripture: "I am convinced that neither death nor life, neither angels nor demons, neither the present nor the future, nor any powers, neither height nor depth, nor anything else in all creation, will be able to separate us from the love of God that is in Christ Jesus our Lord" (Romans 8:38-39).

Favorite Music: Hillsong United

Favorite Books: *Crazy Love* by Francis Chan and anything by Karen Kingsbury!

Favorite Food: Give me a taco with some chips and queso and I'm a happy girl!

Most Embarrassing Moment: When my name was called as one of the top-five contestants at the 2007 Miss America pageant, I slipped on my dress and almost bit the dust—on national television! Thankfully I found my balance, but if you watch the tape you can see how close it was.

Coolest Thing I've Recently Done: Sang the national anthem at NBA game for the Oklahoma City Thunder

Craziest Job: I was a jewelry model on QVC during my year serving as Miss America.

Pet Peeve: Bad drivers...especially when the slower drivers drive in the fast lane

Lauren & Randy

Activities: I love hanging with my hubby, leading worship, spending time with family (especially shopping with my mom and sister!), and walking each day with friends Robin, Sherry, Natalee, and Michelle. I have fun blogging—such a great outlet to share what God places on my heart! I love digging into God's Word. The more I learn, the more I want to learn!

Day I Met Jesus: I grew up in a Christian home so I knew a lot about God, but I didn't have a personal relationship with Him. On July 4, 2008, I gave my life to Christ and began the adventure I'm on right now. I've learned that God is faithful to do extraordinary things with ordinary people like me—if we let Him!

What Robin Says About Lauren: Lauren is even prettier on the inside than the outside. And a lot of people might not know that this girl can sure eat... and never gain a pound! LOL

Getting Connected

Working as a television news reporter is an exciting adventure. Little did I (Robin) know how the reporting assignment to interview Lauren Nelson, Miss America 2007, would change both our lives. A friendship blossomed, and God planted a seed in our hearts. So began the journey that led to the book you are now holding.

God, Girls, and Getting Connected dives into issues that are happening in your life on a daily basis. Do you have trouble spending time in God's Word? Is girl drama an everyday problem? Do you have questions about how relationships work—and what God has to say about them? If so, get ready because no topic is off-limits! We tackle gossip, guys, growing up, and even social media. Find out how God fits into every part of your life!

Each devotion starts with a girl's text message to God. God's response is a text message from His Word, the Bible. We know you're making decisions right now that will shape the rest of your life, and now is the perfect time to ask God the questions on your heart and listen for His answers.

We've broken the devotions into four sections based on the acronym G-I-R-L.

> **"G"** stands for God. This is the starting-off point in discovering God. You'll look at questions like "Who is God?" "Why is it important to be connected to Him?" "How can I rely on God to help me navigate this crazy world I live in?"

> **"I"** stands for identity. As you dig into God's Word, you'll discover that God sees you differently than the world sees you...or even how you see yourself. We pray you will come to know yourself as a daughter of the King!

> **"R"** stands for relationships. Who doesn't need help in this area? Relationships are hard whether you're talking friends, boyfriends, parents, brothers and sisters, or teachers. You'll look at how to

have meaningful, godly relationships and how to respect authority figures. You'll discover keys on how to "date right" and set boundaries in romantic relationships so you're protected and prepared.

"L" stands for life. Do you ever find yourself walking down the same roads in life and continually falling into the same potholes? Maybe the "hole" is a specific choice or action. Maybe it's your friends or the words you say. No matter who you are, there will be potholes in life, so you'll discover ways to avoid them—and survive them if you do fall in.

We're so excited about taking this journey with you! Our prayer is that God's power will be packed into every word and every page of this book. We are praying for you and asking God to open your eyes to the adventure that He has in store for you. Our hope is for you to become a confident woman in Christ, prepared to take on the world with all of its ups and downs. Be assured that you're never alone because God is with you always.

It's time to get connected. Are you ready?

We love you, friend!

Robin
Lauren

Contents

GOD

How cool is a job where one day you get to hang out with a major music star and the next day you are able to ask the vice president of the country a question? The world of television news is exciting indeed! My work as a news anchor has been "on camera" for more than 25 years. I like sharing stories about the famous people I've met and interviewed for my job.

I especially love to tell about the "Greatest Person" I've ever met! My life changed the moment I met *Him*. I've never been the same. That person is Jesus Christ. Who is He? He's the One who gives peace when you're afraid. He makes a pact to never leave your side. And most important, He offers you the chance to have eternal life with Him and in Him. That life-changing experience through Jesus is available to you—all you have to do is ask Him!

God is calling your heart, and He wants you to recognize His ringtone. Let these devotions help you connect to God. You'll be glad you answered His call!

Blessings,
Robin

Faith in the Unseen and Unknown

Emma: "How am I supposed to trust and believe God when I can't see Him?"

God's Text: "So we fix our eyes not on what is seen, but on what is unseen, since what is seen is temporary, but what is unseen is eternal" (2 Corinthians 4:18).

Getting Connected •

When you sit in a chair, you have faith the chair will hold you up. You know this because you can see the chair, you've seen other people sitting in chairs, and you trust that the chair will not break, move, or disappear. It's easy to trust the chair because you can see it and touch it.

If putting your faith in God is difficult because you can't see or touch Him physically, it's time to focus on the *evidence* of God that exists all around you. Think about the sun. Consider how God created this huge, fiery ball to heat and light the earth. Examine the intricate, spectacular flowers in your yard. Stare at your hand and take note of the incredible, loving craftsmanship that went into shaping it and making it purposeful.

One of the most vivid and beautiful pieces of God-evidence is His followers. Ruth, a woman mentioned in the Old Testament, is just one example. She followed her mother-in-law, Naomi, to a land she had never seen. Ruth left her parents, her hometown, and everything she knew to follow a God she didn't know. Ruth saw evidence of God through Naomi. Ruth told Naomi, "Don't urge me to leave you or to turn back from you. Where you go I will go, and where you stay I will stay. Your people will be my people and your God my God" (Ruth 1:16). That showed Ruth's foundation of faith in the one true God!

Today's App: What is stopping you from having faith in God? Look around. Pay special attention to the way God is revealing Himself to you. If you're a believer, are you reflecting God to the world? Share your faith with someone today—not just with words but with actions too.

He Is Your Everything

Samantha: "There is no way God can be all I need Him to be in my life."

God's Text: "God is able to bless you abundantly, so that in all things at all times, having all that you need, you will abound in every good work" (2 Corinthians 9:8).

Getting Connected

Do you have times when you feel incapable of going on? Maybe an illness or the stress and pressure of school gets to you? It's difficult to see past today's trouble. Because of our humanness, we are in a constant state of need. The *only* person who can satisfy that void is God. No matter what we are facing, He is big enough and mighty enough to help us handle it.

Do you know God has more than 70 names? Each one describes a special characteristic of His. Here is a sampling:

Elohim means "creator God." He created you, knitted you together perfectly and uniquely.

El Shaddai means "God all sufficient." He can take care of everything.

Jehovah or *Yahweh* means "I AM." God was here before the creation of the Earth, and He will be here after it is gone.

Jehovah-Jireh means "God the provider." God always gives you what you need.

Jehovah-Rophe means "the God who heals."

Jehovah-Nissi means. "God our banner." God is present and active on the battlefield of life with us.

Jehovah-Shalom means "God our peace." When the world throws us curveball after curveball and we are falling apart, God is our peace.

Jehovah-Tsidkenu means "God our Righteousness." When God looks at us, He sees righteousness because the blood of Jesus Christ covers us. Jesus is our only righteousness.

Jehovah-Shammah means "the Lord is there." God is with us wherever we go and in whatever storm we face.

God can and will provide everything you need. You only have to invite Him to be your Lord and Savior and ask for His help.

Today's App: Hand your life and all your needs and expectations to God. Let Him be your peace, your comfort, your healer, your provider. Tear down the walls and let God come through for you and be your everything.

The Gift

Colleen: "What do I have to do to be a Christian?"

God's Text: "To all who did receive him, to those who believed in his name, he gave the right to become children of God" (John 1:12).

Getting Connected ●

Do you remember asking your parents whether Santa Claus was real? Many parents said, "If you want to receive, you have to believe." If you wanted Christmas presents, you probably decided believing meant receiving! Do you believe Jesus Christ is real? Do you believe His promises are true for you? He wants to give you the best gift you can receive—eternal life. That present, the gift of salvation, is available to you, but you have to ask for it to receive it. One of the most well-known verses in the Bible plainly shares God's best gift to us: "God so loved the world that he gave his one and only Son, that whoever believes in him shall not perish but have eternal life" (John 3:16). Have you made this verse personal to you? Do you believe in Jesus? More importantly, did you ask and receive?

Today's App: Do you remember a time when you prayed and asked God to forgive you of your sins and become the Lord of your life? If not, you can do that right now! There is no "magic" salvation prayer. You just need to talk to God. He wants to hear from you. Here's a prayer to help you:

Dear Lord, I know I am a sinner. I believe You came, died on a cross, and rose from the grave three days later. Please forgive me for my sins. I accept Your wonderful gift of salvation. Thank You for the promise of love and eternal life! In Your name I pray. Amen.

If you prayed this prayer for the first time, please tell someone—especially someone who will help you connect with a Bible-believing church full of people who love Jesus. Welcome to the family of God!

Because I Said So

Kristen: "Why should I listen to God? He's always asking me to do hard or impossible things."

God's Text: "If you love me, keep my commands" (John 14:15).

Getting Connected

When you think of the word "obedience," you might picture your mom pointing her finger at the clothes on your bedroom floor while saying, "Clean up this mess!" or your dad telling you "Take out the trash or you can't go to the movie with your friends." In the dictionary, "obedience" is defined as "dutiful or submissive behavior." Obedience is an *act*. You have a choice when it comes to obeying your parents. You also have a choice when it comes to obeying God. God will not force you to answer His call. He wants your *willing* obedience.

Think about Mary, the mother of Jesus. She was most likely a *teenager* when God sent His angel to tell her she would give birth to Jesus. Can you imagine being told you were going to give birth to the Savior of the world? Even though you were a virgin? Mary surely thought, "How can this be? God is asking the impossible!" Mary chose to obey God. How different history and our lives would be if Mary hadn't been obedient and willing to embrace God's plan.

"The one who keeps God's commands lives in him, and he in them. And this is how we know that he lives in us: We know it by the Spirit he gave us" (1 John 3:24). When you obey God, you are in constant fellowship with Him. Think of it this way—when you obey Him, you get closer to Him. When you are closer to Him, you are made more like Him. When you listen to God and choose to obey Him, He will do amazing things in and through you.

Today's App: Is God knocking on the door of your heart, asking you to do something? Have you been putting off what He is asking you to do? Take some time to pray today. Ask God to show you what He wants you to do and to give you the strength, courage, and confidence to walk forward in obedience. You just might change the world.

Who Should I Ask?

Cherish: "I'm confused. I get so much advice from others that I don't know which way to turn. Everyone has a different opinion. I don't know who to listen to."

God's Text: "Call to me and I will answer you and tell you great and unsearchable things you do not know" (Jeremiah 33:3).

Getting Connected ●

Do you remember sharing secrets with your best friend when you were younger? Through giggles and laughter you nestled close to your friend's ear to tell her the things on your heart. God loves to tell us His secrets too! In fact, He communicates His secrets the same way you used to with your girlfriends—through a whisper. When God speaks to our hearts, He doesn't usually shout. It's in the quiet moments we spend with Him that we hear His voice loud and clear.

When you're making important decisions, it's always wise to get the counsel of friends and relatives, but remember the greatest counsel comes from God. Listen for the "gentle whisper" of God in your heart (1 Kings 19:12). After all, He knows you better than anyone else.

Today's App: Carve out some time to be still before God. Being still doesn't mean you can't move. It just means removing the distractions of life. Turn off your cell phone, get away from the computer, and find a place to be alone with God. Be quiet and wait for Him to speak. God's advice is always right on target.

Why the Bible?

Amy: "Is reading the Bible really that important?"

God's Text: "They are not just idle words for you—they are your life. By them you will live long in the land you are crossing the Jordan to possess" (Deuteronomy 32:47).

Getting Connected

Here is a challenge for the week. Can you spend seven days without using technology? No laptop, no cell phone, no iPod, no playlists? Would you say that is impossible? Do you sometimes wonder if you'd go slightly nuts without technology? If so, you're in good company. Most girls feel the same way.

Do you feel the same way about being connected to God through His Word? While we tremble at the idea of being without our cell phones or computers for one day, it's not uncommon for many believers to go days or even weeks without opening a Bible. Just imagine what your day would be like if you were as passionate about God's Word as you are about using your cell phone, computer, and iPad.

The apostle Paul wrote, "All Scripture is God-breathed and is useful for teaching, rebuking, correcting and training in righteousness, so that the servant of God may be thoroughly equipped for every good work" (2 Timothy 3:16-17). God's Word is your lifeline. Rely on the Lord every minute of your life because without Him you are lifeless. Read the Bible every day, listening for Christ to speak to you. He's the source of all life and joy!

Today's App: Are you using God's Word as your lifeline? Stay connected! Read the Word every day. Going through this devotional will also help you discover timely wisdom from God.

Who Do I Trust?

Courtney: "My friend just told the whole school something that was private between us. I am so sad and disappointed."

God's Text: "The word of God is alive and active. Sharper than any double-edged sword, it penetrates even to dividing soul and spirit, joints and marrow; it judges the thoughts and attitudes of the heart" (Hebrews 4:12).

Getting Connected

How do you know when you can totally trust someone? Whether it is a friend, a boyfriend, a parent, or someone you look up to, can you trust that person with your deepest secrets and know he or she will honor your privacy? Do you watch for people to prove themselves trustworthy before you share your heart and thoughts? While you may endure a few heartaches or disappointments, you will find people who are honest, reliable, and discreet.

There's one thing that is always right and true—God's Word. The Bible has the answers to all of life's tough questions. It will show you the "green light" when you're making right choices and the "red light" when you are doing wrong. You can rely on it even when you don't know what to do.

You can also express yourself honestly to God. He already knows the thoughts and intentions of your heart, but He likes to hear from you. He has proven Himself, and you can trust Him. Isaiah 40:8 says, "The grass withers and the flowers fall, but the word of our God endures forever."

Today's App: Have you been let down in the trust department? List some ways God's Word has been trustworthy in your life.

Don't Mute Me

Hannah: "Does God really hear me?"

God's Text: "Pray in the Spirit on all occasions with all kinds of prayers and requests. With this in mind, be alert and always keep on praying for all the Lord's people" (Ephesians 6:18).

Getting Connected ●

Does it seem strange when you pray to God sometimes? Does it seem awkward that the Creator of the universe wants to have a conversation with you? Even if it does, God's Word encourages you to pray...and never stop.

Here's a fun exercise to help you discover what to pray for and why prayer is so amazing. Hold up your hand and let your fingers guide your prayer:

- *Thumb:* When your thumb is "up," it represents praise—acknowledging who God is and His attributes.

- *Index finger:* When you point this finger, you can point to all the ways you are thankful to the Lord.

- *Middle finger:* As you point with your index finger, your middle finger is pointing back to you. Remember to confess your sins and ask for forgiveness.

- *Ring finger:* This is a sign of adoration. Just as a wedding ring is an outward sign of a spouse's adoration, your ring finger can remind you to love your heavenly Father.

- *Pinky finger:* This is your "petition" finger. It's the smallest finger and a reminder that even your smallest needs are important to God.

Today's App: Use the hand example to guide your prayers today. Even if you feel "all thumbs" at first, let your heart guide your praises and requests to the Lord.

Your Gifts

Jordan: "I feel like a nobody. How can God ever use me?"

God's Text: "There are different kinds of gifts, but the same Spirit distributes them" (1 Corinthians 12:4).

Getting Connected

Every person and every creation is unique and has special purposes. Think about all the different types of animals. Some animals run, some hop, some swim, some fly. But they are all part of God's creation and design. Each young woman is designed perfectly by God to do certain things. Even before God created you, He had a master plan designed for you. He has unique ways for you to serve Him so that He will receive the glory and your life will have purpose and meaning. You are a one-of-a-kind masterpiece made by God!

The apostle Paul wrote, "We are God's handiwork, created in Christ Jesus to do good works, which God prepared in advance for us to do" (Ephesians 2:10). This means nothing happens in your life that is meaningless. God will use *every opportunity* to shape and mold you into the special person He created you to be. He gave you intelligence, interests, talents, gifts, emotions, and, yes, even opportunities to make mistakes so you will grow strong. Thank God today for the way He created you!

Today's App: Have you ever taken a spiritual gift test? There are many different kinds available. Check it out. Or ask your mom and dad what they think your special gifts are. Then sit down and make a list of all the things you like to do. These are your interests. Ask God to help you serve Him with your whole heart in the areas of your gifts and interests.

Up, Down, Right, or Left?

Elizabeth: "I feel lost, like I can't find my way in life."

God's Text: "Your word [LORD,] is a lamp for my feet, a light on my path" (Psalm 119:105).

Getting Connected ●

Have you ever felt lost or headed in the wrong direction? Have you ever panicked and looked at your GPS for directions or had to ask someone how to get back to familiar territory? Being lost is not a good feeling—especially when you're in the middle of nowhere. You may feel the same way about life and the choices you face. Which college will you go to? What career will you choose? Who will you date? Will you marry?

It's tough when you're faced with so many choices, but remember, God has provided a map! His Word is the best and ultimate guide for life.

Today's App: Imagine driving a car at night without headlights. That would be pretty scary, right? But that's exactly what your life would be like without God's Word illuminating your way. Memorize Psalm 25:4: "Show me your ways, LORD, teach me your paths."

Stinkin' Thinkin'

Amanda: "I want to do what is right, but being mean sometimes seems easier."

God's Text: "The Lord detests the thoughts of the wicked, but gracious words are pure in his sight" (Proverbs 15:26).

Getting Connected ●

Do you ever find yourself plotting revenge against someone who hurt you? It may feel satisfying at first, but underneath that satisfaction is deception. When you plan to harm someone else or cause some kind of destruction, you are the one who really gets hurt. Why? Because you're taking your focus off God and His values and, instead, focusing on what your "flesh" wants.

Getting your feelings hurt is no laughing matter. Emotional hurts caused by a close friend are not only devastating to your heart but they also may be dangerous to your head. Why? Because your anger might lead to "stinkin' thinkin'" that clouds good judgment and masks God's guidance. The Message paraphrases Proverbs 15:26 this way: "God can't stand evil scheming, but he puts words of grace and beauty on display."

How you respond to hurt is up to you. You have a choice. Instead of seeking revenge, ask God to place the right words and actions in your thoughts and then follow through on what He says. Now you don't have to think twice about getting even because you're letting God's love rule your heart.

Today's App: Do you need to eliminate some "stinkin' thinkin'"? Talk to God now and ask Him to help you recognize when you need to speak words of grace and beauty.

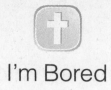

I'm Bored

Tiffanie: "Sometimes church seems so boring. Is it really important for me to go?"

God's Text: "Let us consider how we may spur one another on toward love and good deeds, not giving up meeting together, as some are in the habit of doing, but encouraging one another—and all the more as you see the Day approaching" (Hebrews 10:24-25).

Getting Connected ●

After Jesus' resurrection on a Sunday, many believers in the early church gathered for worship on that day of the week instead of the Jewish Sabbath of Saturday. Sunday became the traditional Christian "Lord's Day." Whether Christians worship on Saturday or Sunday, it is a day to encourage one another, especially during times of persecution. At church, believers share God's Word, sing praise songs to God, pray for one another, and often eat together. For many, "the Lord's day" is a time to worship with their immediate families, but if your family doesn't go to church, you can worship with your "church family."

Although the style of worship where you attend church may seem boring at times, remember you're there to worship and learn more about God—and He is never boring!

Deciding to attend church on a regular basis will help you develop a lifestyle of faithfulness and grow in your faith and knowledge.

Today's App: Make God a priority, not an afterthought. Following God will make your life more exciting! Next Sunday, focus on *Who* you are worshipping, not on how the meetings are conducted. Put your heart and soul into worshipping God at church, and you will discover how exciting it can be.

Is Opportunity Knocking?

Lily: "I feel like God is telling me to share my faith with my friend, but I'm too nervous. I'm afraid it will make her mad or make her not like me."

God's Text: "Work at telling others the Good News, and fully carry out the ministry God has given you" (2 Timothy 4:5 NLT).

Getting Connected ●

As a Christian, you get to experience the awesome privileges and joys of knowing God every day. He not only offers you salvation, but He also invites you into an intimate relationship with Him. You can talk to God and bring your troubles to Him. He wants to know *everything* about you—the good, the bad, and the ugly! Nothing will shock Him or make Him love you less. He is your best friend who listens, offers wise advice, and loves you no matter what. Wouldn't you like everyone to have that? Especially your friends and family?

The apostle Paul was a big-time persecutor of Christians until God spoke to him on the road to Damascus and even blinded him to get his attention. God arranged for Ananias, a devout man, to heal Paul so he could become a powerful Christian and preach the gospel to Gentiles and Jews around the world (in person and through his letters included in the Bible). Paul never backed down from sharing about his life-changing experience. His world had been so rocked by God, he *had* to tell people!

Today's App: Is there someone God has placed on your heart to talk to about Jesus? Don't miss an opportunity to share your belief in Christ. Pray about the doors God opens for you. Ask Him for confidence, courage, and boldness. And don't worry! God will help you know what to say.

Easy Street?

Grace: "Sometimes the Christian life is so hard. Why don't my troubles just go away?"

God's Text: "We are hard pressed on every side, but not crushed; perplexed, but not in despair; persecuted, but not abandoned; struck down, but not destroyed" (2 Corinthians 4:8-9).

Getting Connected ●

A big myth is that when we become Christians life gets easy. Some people assume—or hope—that as soon as they become believers their problems will disappear. Think about this for a second. If we had zero worries about school, boyfriends, parents, or drama with other people, when would we seek God? Imagine missing out on God's incredible ability to change, heal, and empower our lives and circumstances!

Let's dismiss the myth and accept the even better truth. When we are Christians, our hope, power, and protection come from knowing our loving God and trusting Him to walk with us through the difficulties, heartaches, and trials.

In God's text today the apostle Paul is talking about the hardships *all* people face, especially Christians. But he doesn't stop there. He speaks of hope and resilience. He reminds us that life is hard but not impossible. God is on our side! If God brings us to a difficult circumstance, He will bring us through it.

Today's App: Face today's troubles with a warrior mentality. Realize when you come toe-to-toe with adversity that God is on your side, battling right there with you!

The Great Eraser

Rachel: "I have done so many things I regret. Last night I went way too far with my boyfriend. Will God forgive me—and still love me?"

God's Text: "'Come now, let us settle the matter,' says the LORD. 'Though your sins are like scarlet, they shall be as white as snow; though they are red as crimson, they shall be like wool'" (Isaiah 1:18).

Getting Connected

Picture this. You're wearing an amazing white outfit to a special dinner at your favorite Italian restaurant with friends. As you reach for your water glass, you bump a plate of spaghetti onto your lap. Those white pants aren't so white anymore. No matter how many times you wash them, those pants are ruined. Sin initially stains us just like that marinara sauce. Thankfully, God has the most powerful eraser when it comes to removing sin.

Do you know the story of Rahab? She was a prostitute and resident of Jericho, a city full of wicked and pagan people. Rahab's life was filled with many stains, but God brought her out of her sin and into a relationship with Him. Not only did He redeem her, but God allowed Rahab the privilege of being one of Jesus' ancestors. She is one of the women in the lineage of Jesus.

No matter how many times you stumble and mess up, God has a never-ending supply of grace. He is faithful to wash away your sins, no matter what is in your past. All you have to do is ask Him for forgiveness.

When God miraculously cleans your heart, you are changed forever! You will experience a deep, great desire to walk closer with Him and further away from sin.

Today's App: Is there sin in your life that you need to repent of (renounce) and ask forgiveness for? Tell God you're sorry and ask Him to forgive you. He is faithful to erase your sins no matter how many or what they are. He can make what is scarlet become as white as snow!

All We Need Is Love

Whitney: "I don't feel like anyone loves me. My parents never pay attention to me, and my girlfriends talk about me behind my back. Does God love me?"

God's Text: "See what great love the Father has lavished on us, that we should be called children of God! And that is what we are! The reason the world does not know us is that it did not know him" (1 John 3:1).

Getting Connected

What is love? That's a pretty broad question, isn't it? Have you ever thought about it? There can be lots of answers to this question. Magazines say love is physical attraction and even sex. Your friends might say love is the sensation of butterflies in the stomach when you meet a special guy. Your parents may say love is choosing not to harm your little brother when he is annoying you. There are all sorts of answers to this question. But what does the Bible say about love?

The greatest statement of love is found in John 3:16: "God so loved the world that he gave his one and only Son, that whoever believes in him shall not perish but have eternal life." Love is a choice. God chose us. He wants to have a personal relationship with each one of us. Because He loves us, He sent His only Son, Jesus, to save us. And out of love, Jesus died on the cross for us. Our God is an awesome God. No matter where we go, what we do, or how many times we fall short, God's love is always available to us. What a gracious gift! And all we have to do is say yes and receive it.

Today's App: Are you struggling with feeling unloved? Even when you might be disappointed by others, God does not and will not disappoint. He loved you yesterday, He loves you today, and He will love you tomorrow! Praise His name and feel His love!

Absent or Present?

Tasha: "I try so hard to hear God's voice. I wonder if He even hears me? He doesn't speak to my heart anymore."

God's Text: "How long, LORD? Will you forget me forever? How long will you hide your face from me? How long must I wrestle with my thoughts and day after day have sorrow in my heart? How long will my enemy triumph over me?" (Psalm 13:1-2).

Getting Connected

Have you ever struggled to hear God's voice? Do you feel disappointed or lonely because He's not answering? You are not alone. Don't be discouraged, friend. God has a purpose in this time of your life. Let Psalm 27:14 encourage you: "Wait for the LORD; be strong and take heart and wait for the LORD." Even though it is hard to understand right now, God is stirring up a special purpose in you that is greater than anything you can dream.

In the Old Testament, we can read about Joseph, who was in prison for 13 years for something he didn't do. Such a devastating situation leads to a lot of questions and confusion about God's presence and love. Yet God was with Joseph. God's plan was divine and beyond Joseph's immediate understanding. Joseph, the same person who was sold into slavery as a boy by his brothers, was exalted by God to be second in command over Egypt (Genesis 41:43). Even prison couldn't separate Joseph from God's great purpose and presence.

Keep forging ahead when it seems like God is silent. He's still working! He will never leave you or forsake you (Hebrews 13:5). So even though it feels like He is absent now, you can trust that He is still with you and working out His good and perfect plan for your life.

Today's App: Why not pray this prayer?

> *Dear God, please use this time in my life to develop persistence and patience in me. I want to hear Your voice and do Your will. Thank You for being with me always. Help me feel Your presence. I want to live in a way that pleases and honors You. In Jesus' name. Amen.*

Hopeful or Hopeless?

Kenzie: "I feel so hopeless. I want to believe I can overcome this, but I feel so incapable."

God's Text: "Be strong and take heart, all you who hope in the LORD" (Psalm 31:24).

Getting Connected

First some quick questions: Do you consider yourself hopeful or hopeless? Are you an optimist or a pessimist? No matter how you answered those questions, there are times when we all feel hopeless. It's easy to get down on ourselves when we fall short of what the people around us and the media tell us about how we should look and what we should be doing. Can you relate?

It's a good thing there is good news! There is a Greater Power working in you—a power no darkness or negative message can overcome. It's the Holy Spirit. Whether you're in a season of sadness or depression, you can always have hope. Jesus said, "I will ask the Father, and he will give you another advocate to help you and be with you forever" (John 14:16).

Today's App: Here's a great prayer:

Lord, help me believe wholeheartedly in the plan You have for my life. Give me the strength to fight off any negative influences. Show me Your plans for me and sustain my hope as I grow into them. In Your name I pray. Amen.

Instructions

Angela: "My friends tease me because I read my Bible all the time. It hurts my feelings!"

God's Text: "Whoever loves discipline loves knowledge, but whoever hates correction is stupid" (Proverbs 12:1).

Getting Connected ●

To pass a test at school, you have to study by reviewing the material. The effort and amount of time you spend learning is usually reflected in the type of grades you receive. The same can be said when it comes to understanding God's promises and plans. He wants to guide your life. He wants you to know Him. And to do that, you have to study His Word.

The Bible is God's instruction manual for your life. It is your most valuable asset. If you know it well, it will prepare you for whatever comes your way. People who don't know Jesus won't understand why you want to know Him better. First Corinthians 3:18-19 says, "Do not deceive yourselves. If any of you think you are wise by the standards of this age, you should become 'fools' so that you may become wise. For the wisdom of this world is foolishness in God's sight."

Ask the Holy Spirit to speak to you as you read God's Word. He will guide you and prepare you for the day. "Blessed are those who find wisdom, those who gain understanding" (Proverbs 3:13).

Today's App: Praise God for providing His manual for your life! Pick a time of day when you can spend 5 to 15 minutes meeting with God and reading His Word. You'll be glad you did! His wisdom and promises will fill you. And those friends who don't know why you read the Bible may be the ones who seek your advice and help.

Yes, No, or Wait?

Kylie: "I've prayed and prayed about this decision, and I feel like God isn't hearing me. Maybe He doesn't care about the little things."

God's Text: "Do you not know? Have you not heard? The LORD is the ever-lasting God, the Creator of the ends of the earth. He will not grow tired or weary, and his understanding no one can fathom" (Isaiah 40:28).

Getting Connected

Do you ever feel like your prayers hit the ceiling and go no further? You wait patiently, but time drags on and there is no answer from God? You wonder, "Where is God?" You have a choice to make. Are you going to believe what you *feel* or what you *know* to be true about God? Romans 8:28 says, "We *know* that in all things God works for the good of those who love him, who have been called according to His purpose."

Why is it good to wait on God? Isaiah 40:31 says "Those who hope in the LORD will renew their strength. They will soar on wings like eagles; they will run and not grow weary, they will walk and not be faint." So keep praying. Keep setting aside time to talk and listen to God. You will hear from Him! And when you do, He may be saying "yes," He may be saying "no," or He may be saying "wait and be patient." How precious is the Lord that He chooses to bless you no matter what His answer is. Don't worry if God is telling you to wait for His answer. Remember His promise: He will never leave you nor forsake you. He loves you no matter what!

Today's App: Are you waiting for an answer from the Lord? Don't rush your response. Patiently wait, resting in His time frame. Trust Him completely, knowing that whether His answer is yes, no, or wait, He wants only the best for you.

Trusting God

Ginnie: "I love the Lord, but I choose to spend my time on schoolwork. My grades are my ticket to a good life of purpose. If I study, there is nothing I can't do!"

God's Text: "Such is the destiny of all who forget God; so perishes the hope of the godless. What they trust in is fragile; what they rely on is a spider's web. They lean on the web, but it gives way; they cling to it, but it does not hold" (Job 8:13-15).

Getting Connected ●

Can you relate to Ginnie's concern? We know the Lord saved us and that we are to put our trust in Him alone. But we're also told constantly to trust other people, other things, and even ourselves. It can be so tempting to do because we often see and experience immediate results. But only God knows everything. God never makes mistakes. People mess up—even parents. They're human. Romans 3:23 says, "All have sinned and fall short of the glory of God."

Proverbs 3:5-6 gives great advice: "Trust in the LORD with all your heart and lean not on your own understanding; in all your ways submit to him, and he will make your paths straight." What a thought! The Almighty God of the universe is asking for your trust. He wants to direct you personally. It doesn't get any better than that!

Today's App: So can you trust God with the big assignment called "Your Life"? The answer is always yes! Are you relying on your looks or brains to get by? Looks eventually fade, and our brainpower is limited. Every human makes mistakes. Trust is built by spending time with someone. Spend time with God and His Word regularly. Ask Him to show you how to rely on Him even more.

Joy

Stacy: "Every day it seems like someone is telling me a new rule for how to live! What is the truth?"

God's Text: "'Of all the commandments, which is the most important?' [Jesus answered,] 'The most important one...is this: "Hear, O Israel: the Lord our God, the Lord is one. Love the Lord your God with all your heart and with all your soul and with all your mind and with all your strength." The second is this: "Love your neighbor as yourself." There is no commandment greater than these'" (Mark 12:28-31).

Getting Connected ●

A kindergarten teacher shared a secret for success that teaches us all a great lesson or two. Her classroom revolved around one rule: J-O-Y. It's an acronym for "**J**esus first, **O**thers second, **Y**ourself third." Each year she told her five-year-old students that if they follow that truth, everyone would have a much better year. That truth fits our lives today too.

Everyone wants to be happy. But do you know there is a difference between happiness and joy? You might look for happiness through the "things" you have—clothes, gadgets, popularity, and that list could go on and on. Do you ever get wrapped up in the mentality of "It's all about me"? If you think stuff will make you happy, remember that everyone leaves this world exactly how they entered it—with nothing. It is not wrong to want nice things, but remember that *temporary* things only bring *temporary* happiness.

Joy is something Jesus says leads to *eternal* happiness. Psalm 4:7 says, "You have given me greater joy" (NLT). God's riches will always trump material riches. When you focus on Jesus first and other people second, you can't help but experience the *you* God had in mind when He created you for His kingdom.

Today's App: Are you living a God-first life? If not, what priorities do you need to change or rearrange to get there? Ask God to show you what He wants you to do today. Live J-O-Y and watch it open doors to God's heart, to helping other people, and to happiness and contentment.

Righteous Jealousy?

Abby: "Why is God described as jealous? I thought jealousy was a bad thing."

God's Text: "I am jealous for you with a godly jealousy. I promised you to one husband, to Christ, so that I might present you as a pure virgin to him" (2 Corinthians 11:2).

Getting Connected

You know the jealous type—those who get mad if someone else has something they don't have. Jealousy sure can mess up friendships! Being jealous *of* someone is a bad thing, and it can have negative effects on how you view and engage with God and yourself. Ungodly jealousy breeds anger, resentment, and bitterness, which takes a toll on your relationships and your health. Proverbs 14:30 says, "A heart at peace gives life to the body, but envy rots the bones."

Do you know there is another kind of jealousy? A good kind? Being jealous *for* someone is a "righteous" jealousy.

In God's text message today, He reveals another aspect of who He is. God is a jealous God. Not jealous *of* us, but jealous *for* us. Think of it this way. Someday, when you get married, you will want your husband to love you—and only you. You'll want all of his love and affection, not just part of it. In the same way, God wants all of us—not just part of us. He wants us to give our whole selves to Him and no one else.

So instead of being jealous *of* people, how about being jealous *for* people? Be jealous *for* them by wanting them to know Christ and have an intimate relationship with Him like you do.

Today's App: When was the last time you were broken and sad for a friend or family member who didn't have a personal relationship with Jesus? Ask God to show you someone you can be jealous *for* and how you can help that person get to know Christ.

Come Hungry, Leave Full

Mallory: "I have to be honest—sometimes I don't want to read my Bible."

God's Text: "Blessed are those who hunger and thirst for righteousness, for they will be filled" (Matthew 5:6).

Getting Connected

Hopefully there has never been a moment in your life when you didn't have enough food to eat. But have you experienced a time after school or at the end of a sporting event when you said you were starving? So you raided the kitchen pantry and devoured anything and everything you found. It didn't really matter what was there because it all tasted really good.

There are times like that spiritually as well. Your appetite for God and His Word should be constantly growing. You need to be searching the cabinets of Scripture and letting the contents fill you with the promises of God's will for your life. When you are motivated to seek Him, God will give you the spiritual food you need to satisfy your hunger. Revelation 7:17 says, "The Lamb at the center of the throne will be their shepherd; 'he will lead them to springs of living water. And God will wipe away every tear from their eyes.'"

Anytime you feel unsatisfied—hungry for someone to care about you and understand you, go to the Word of God. It is the *best* meal of the day.

Today's App: Are you intentional about a well-balanced meal with God? What kind of effort are you giving to staying spiritually fit? Ask God to give you a hunger to spend time with Him and His Word.

Pleasing People vs. Pleasing God

Ally: "I tend to be a people pleaser. Is that bad?"

God's Text: "Am I now trying to win the approval of human beings, or of God? Or am I trying to please people? If I were still trying to please people, I would not be a servant of Christ" (Galatians 1:10).

Getting Connected ●

The issue of pleasing both God and your friends can be a struggle. Have you ever been with friends and wanted to speak up for what is right, but you kept silent because it was easier? God didn't create the world so that you'd always be comfortable. He made it so that you might live to know Him better and share His love with others. For some people, this involves reading the Bible with strangers or going door to door to spread the Good News about Jesus.

How do you please God? Your life and actions speak louder than your words ever can. When you choose to do what is right in God's eyes, you'll soon discover that is far more pleasing and satisfying than any momentary approval given by a group of friends. Your friends will change throughout your life, but God never will! So please the One who will never leave you and who will bring you lasting peace.

Today's App: Take time today to evaluate whether you tend to please your friends and family instead of God. Choose to make God your new top priority. Keep your head up and be willing to speak up for what is right. The results are worth it! Your efforts to please the King of the universe will bring you so much peace. He will give you strength and comfort. You need only to trust Him.

It Comes Down to This

Carly: "The Old Testament is so confusing. I give up trying to understand it."

God's Text: "Love the Lᴏʀᴅ your God with all your heart and with all your soul and with all your strength" (Deuteronomy 6:5).

Getting Connected ●

Everything that is written in the Old Testament is an example for us to live by. It is a love letter from God. Yes, some of it is a little hard to understand. But have you considered that He had it written that way so we would have to read it over and over, spending more time in His presence? And the more time we spend with Him, the more we love Him. This relates to the greatest commandment, as Jesus explained to His disciples. He said, "'Love the Lord your God with all your heart and with all your soul and with all your mind.' This is the first and greatest commandment" (Matthew 22:37-38). Loving God means spending time with Him and studying His Word...even when it's hard.

Today's App: What are you doing to show God how much you love Him?

Great Expectations

Lacy: "I believe God performed miracles back in Bible times, but I'm not sure He still works like that. I believe He can, I just don't know if He does or will."

God's Text: "Jesus replied, 'Truly I tell you, if you have faith and do not doubt, not only can you do what was done to the fig tree, but also you can say to this mountain, "Go, throw yourself into the sea," and it will be done. If you believe, you will receive whatever you ask for in prayer'" (Matthew 21:21-22).

Getting Connected ●

The Bible is packed with examples of God performing miracles. There's the parting of the Red Sea, the boy David beating the giant Goliath, the walls of Jericho falling down. These are examples of God showing up and working in awesome, mighty ways. There is one common denominator in all of the miracles mentioned in the Bible: The people God used in the situations *expected* God to show up. They didn't just hope He would work the problem out. Can you imagine how the Israelites would have reacted if Moses had doubted God when they arrived at the Red Sea? But Moses didn't hesitate. He said, "Do not be afraid. Stand firm and you will see the deliverance the LORD will bring you today" (Exodus 14:13). Moses knew God would take care of them, and he *expected* God to act. God showed up in a big way and the waters parted!

When we seek the Lord and believe and expect Him to work, God will show up in a big way and people will see and be encouraged by our faith. God is still in the miracle-working business. We just need to expect them to happen.

Today's App: When life is difficult, spend time praying. Ask God to work in a special way in the situation and to give you a heart of expectation for His deliverance.

Whom Should I Believe?

Mariah: "How do I know when I'm hearing the voice of God?"

God's Text: "Be alert and of sober mind. Your enemy the devil prowls around like a roaring lion looking for someone to devour. Resist him, standing firm in the faith, because you know that the family of believers throughout the world is undergoing the same kind of sufferings" (1 Peter 5:8-9).

Getting Connected

In the midst of the clutter that surrounds us, the voice of God can be hard to hear. When you add school, friends, family time, and work, it is even easier to see how His voice can get crowded out in our lives. The truth is that our enemy, Satan, does a good job of interfering with our ability to hear and understand the voice that matters the most to us—God's.

Satan fills our minds with lies about what true beauty is. He reminds us of our sin even after we've repented and been forgiven by God. Satan tries to trip us up and confuse us so we will crumble under the weight of his lies. But we don't have to listen to the devil!

In God's text message today, Peter warns us of our enemy, but he also gives us advice on how to fight back. Our weapon against Satan's attacks is *firm faith*. We must *choose to believe what God says* about us instead of listening to Satan's lies. For instance, the devil tries to plant the idea in our heads that beauty is unattainable, but God's Word says, "Your royal husband delights in your beauty; honor him, for he is your lord" (Psalm 45:11 NLT). Satan would have us believe that God is keeping a running tally of our sins, but God's Word says, "For as high as the heavens are above the earth, so great is his love for those who fear him; as far as the east is from the west, so far has he removed our transgressions from us" (Psalm 103:11-12). We can quiet the enemy of our souls with our firm faith in the truth of what God says about us!

Today's App: Do you have trouble knowing what the voice of God sounds like? Ask God to help you recognize His voice. Ask Him to help you ignore the lies of the enemy and concentrate on God's truths about who you are.

Confusion Dilemma

Minnie: "I've been praying about making a decision. One minute I feel like I am hearing one answer, and then in the next moment I feel like I'm hearing the opposite answer. I'm so confused!"

God's Text: "Now if any of you lacks wisdom, he should ask God, who gives to all generously and without criticizing, and it will be given to him. But let him ask in faith without doubting" (James 1:5-6 HCSB).

Getting Connected ●

There is one thing you can count on when you have a decision to make: God is *not* the author of confusion. How many times have we all been there? There is an important decision to make and our head says, "Do it this way," while our hearts say, "No, do it another way." Look again at Minnie's comment. Can you catch why she is so unsettled about making her decision? She is asking God for help, but she is basing her decision on how she *feels*. Feelings can be a confusion trap. Just like the wind changes from one direction to another, so can our emotions.

So what can you do? If you have a decision to make, you can rely on God to help you! "Trust in the Lord with all your heart and lean not on your own understanding; in all your ways submit to him, and he will make your paths straight" (Proverbs 3:5-6). God's Word is your lifeline! When in doubt about what to do, look to God's Word for wisdom and pray. Ask God to make it clear what His will is for you. Keep your eyes open to see His way and your ears ready to hear Him speak to your heart.

Today's App: Remember to guard against being double-minded. God's Word is your stability when the tough decisions come. Trust God's Word and wisdom instead of your feelings.

Gag Reflex

Jana: "I'm not clear on what sin is. Do you know?"

God's Text: "Hate what is evil; cling to what is good" (Romans 12:9).

Getting Connected

Do you have a sensitive gag reflex? Not to try to make you lose your last meal, but do you know what a gag reflex is? It's that instinctive reaction your body has if you're choking…if something goes down the airway instead of the esophagus. The gag reflex is what makes you heave or throw up. It sounds gross, but God designed it for your protection.

Do you have a gag reflex when it comes to sin? Think about everything that has been poured into your life. Are there some things that may need to be choked out? How about gossip, worry, fear, plotting revenge, lying to your parents, or even watching shows and movies that are inappropriate? Is there anything else you should decide to keep out of your heart, mind, and soul?

Today's verse says to hate evil and cling to what is good. One definition for "cling" is "to hold on tightly." Think how a small child holds tightly to her parent's hand when crossing a street. Now do the same with God. Never let go of His Word. You will never choke on His food—it tastes great and goes down smoothly.

Today's App: Some people's gag reflexes are so sensitive that even if something stinks they gag. Ask God to make your instinctive reaction this sensitive when it comes to sin so you will know what is evil and what is good.

A True Christian

Annalee: "I'm a good girl and do nice things for people. Doesn't that mean I'm a Christian?"

God's Text: "If you confess with your mouth, 'Jesus is Lord,' and believe in your heart that God raised him from the dead, you will be saved" (Romans 10:9).

Jesus replied, "Anyone who loves me will obey my teaching. My Father will love them, and we will come to them and make our home with them" (John 14:23).

Getting Connected

Many people believe just like Annalee, that being good and doing nice things for people makes them Christians. In today's verse, the Bible makes it very clear what it takes to be known as a true Christ follower.

God created all of us to have fellowship with Him. The Bible says He loved us so much He sent Jesus, His Son, to die on the cross to pay for our sins and to give us the free gift of eternal life. God's love is available to everyone, but receiving it is not automatic. There is one thing that separates all of us from the love of God—our sin. Before we could approach our holy God, our sin had to be paid for. This is why God the Father sent Jesus to the cross—He died to pay for our sins. The free gift He holds out to us is eternal life—to never again be separated from Him!

So how can you accept the payment of your sins (salvation) and the free gift of eternal life? Acknowledge you are a sinner and repent from your sins. Tell Jesus you receive His gift of salvation by making Him your Lord and Savior. Believe God raised Jesus from the dead just like Scripture says He did.

Accepting Jesus really is life-changing! Once you've done that, you can fellowship with Him 24 hours a day, 7 days a week for the rest of your life. He sends the Holy Spirit to live in your heart to guide you and show you the best path for your life. You have Jesus Christ as your Savior, the Holy

Spirit as your guide, and God as your heavenly Father. People will see the joy of the Lord in your heart and life. You are a true Christian!

Today's App: If you haven't accepted Jesus as Lord of your life, why not reach out to Him today? You only need to confess your sins and receive Him as your Lord and Savior, and you will be His forever! Here is a simple prayer you can use if you'd like:

> *Dear Jesus, I know I am a sinner. I believe You came to earth as a man, died on a cross for my sins, and rose from the dead three days later. Please forgive my sins. I accept Your wonderful gift of salvation. Thank You for Your love and eternal life with You. In Your name I pray. Amen.*

Make Yourself at Home

Terry: "I'm not comfortable sharing the dark parts of who I am. I would rather not talk about it, even with God."

God's Text: "You have searched me, LORD, and you know me. You know when I sit and when I rise; you perceive my thoughts from afar. You discern my going out and my lying down; you are familiar with all my ways. Before a word is on my tongue you, LORD, know it completely" (Psalm 139:1-4).

Getting Connected

Going on vacation and staying in a hotel room for a few nights is fun. There are lots of perks. Someone makes your bed for you, fresh towels are provided daily, and you have access to the pool. But after the initial thrill, you might crave your own bed in your own room. No matter how hard you try, that hotel never feels quite like home.

Have you thought about whether God feels at home in your heart? Is He like a guest in a hotel or is He in the comfort of a warm, inviting place? When you are at home, you are comfortable. You watch TV in your pajamas, have free rein to the refrigerator, and can go anywhere anytime. If God is truly at home in your heart, He has free rein and unlimited access to all the rooms in your heart, including the closet where you hide the dirty laundry. As today's message from God points out, He already knows all about you. He is just waiting for you to open your heart and invite Him in.

Today's App: God longs to be at home in your heart. He wants to be a *resident*, not just an occasional guest. Ask Him to take over your heart and maybe even do a little housecleaning. You'll be glad you did!

Time for a Tune-up

Elise: "When I read God's Word, my life looks nothing like what it says."

God's Text: "All Scripture is God-breathed and is useful for teaching, rebuking, correcting and training in righteousness, so that the servant of God may be thoroughly equipped for every good work" (2 Timothy 3:16-17).

Getting Connected

When you have a car, you need to take it to an auto shop every 3000 miles. You get the oil changed, the tires rotated and balanced, and they do a maintenance check to make sure everything is running smoothly. Just like your car needs this regular tune-up, your life needs to be checked out to make sure everything is running right. The mechanic has a list of requirements to test the car against, and you have the Bible to serve as your measure to see if your life is on the right track or needs to be rebalanced.

We are blessed to have the Bible as our manual on how to do life God's way. On every page there are instructions about living a lifestyle that is worthy of the name "Christian." In God's text today we read that the Bible is good for teaching and correcting. As you read God's Word, ask, "Do my actions match up with the Bible?" If not, ask God to help you rebalance your life and get back on the right road.

Today's App: Does your life need a tune-up? There's good news! God is a master mechanic, and He is ready to fine-tune your life. Measure your life against God's Word, and ask God to help you make sure your heart and mind are in alignment with His will.

IDENTITY

My life changed when Mario Lopez called my name as the new Miss America in 2007. I went from being a normal, small-town girl to a young woman traveling the country, meeting exciting people, speaking to groups, and living a life that thousands of girls dream about. It was easy to be dazzled by the crown, the beautiful gowns, and the attention that came with the title. But I learned that "Miss America" was not who I was but what I did.

It is easy for us to base all of our identity on what we *do,* whether that is being a cheerleader, a basketball player, first chair in the band, a good student, or even Miss America. But those activities can be gone as quickly as they began. The world says we are defined by what we have, who we date, the clothes we wear, and what we look like. But what does God say about who we are? Ephesians 2:10 says, "We are God's handiwork, created in Christ Jesus to do good works, which God prepared in advance for us to do." When we look to God, we find our true, lasting identity based on who He created us to be.

Love,
Lauren

The Answer You Don't Want

Chelsea: "What do I do if I've gotten involved with the wrong crowd?"

God's Text: "When I brought your ancestors out of Egypt and spoke to them, I did not just give them commands about burnt offerings and sacrifices, but I gave them this command: Obey me, and I will be your God and you will be my people. Walk in obedience to all I command you, that it may go well with you" (Jeremiah 7:22-23).

Getting Connected

Have you asked God a question and received a pretty clear answer, but it wasn't what you expected or hoped for? For instance, are you holding on to relationships that go against His desires for you? Is there a friend who's pulling you down spiritually instead of challenging you to walk closer to the Lord? Getting a tough answer from God can be difficult, but acting on the answer might be harder.

So how do you respond? Looking for friends is a hard task to do any day of the week. You have a choice. Will you ignore what God is telling you or will you respond in obedience? The best answer? Trust God. He will be your best friend and your most consistent friend. He will never leave you. Trust Him with everything, including the times when His answers might not be exactly what you want to hear.

Whew! What a relief. You don't have to debate, just follow what He says.

P.S. Don't forget to pray for the friend who is pulling you down. God loves her too.

Today's App: Has God told you no lately? How did you respond? What steps can you take today to obey and trust Him even more? Is there someone you need to pray for today?

Time for God

Paige: "I don't know the best way to spend time with God. Help!"

God's Text: "All Scripture is God-breathed and is useful for teaching, rebuking, correcting and training in righteousness, so that the servant of God may be thoroughly equipped for every good work" (2 Timothy 3:16-17).

Getting Connected

You want to spend time with God and learn how to walk with Him, but where do you begin? Start by reading God's Word every day. God is very clear. He has given you His Word, which is an all-inclusive instruction manual that comes alive when you have a relationship with Him and study His teachings.

Here are some questions to consider: Do you seek God by reading His Word on a routine basis? Do you have a specific time each day that you meet with Him? What can you do during your time with God? First, read Scripture. Whether it's one verse or a chapter, take time to read and really think about the message God has for you. Spend time talking to God in prayer. Chat with Him just like you are talking to a friend. He really wants to know what's on your heart. Take time to be silent before God. When He speaks to your heart, be ready to hear Him. While He won't speak in an audible voice, you will sense His directions by expectantly waiting on Him. Relationships require spending time with someone. Make it a habit to spend time each day with God and the instruction manual He provides.

Today's App: Determine a specific time and place where you will read God's Word and talk to Him every day. Be consistent! Develop the habit of placing His Word in your heart.

Refined Through Trials

Emma: "Nothing is going my way."

God's Text: "[God] knows the way that I take; when he has tested me, I will come forth as gold" (Job 23:10).

Getting Connected ●

Ever feel like things are not going your way? Whether you're struggling through chemistry, not getting the score you wanted on the ACT, or not making the dance squad, life throws you curveballs regularly. These are all called "tests," and God allows them to be part of your life so you will be fully dependent on Him. His desire is for you to trust Him in the tough times and to learn through difficult circumstances. Don't wish away your hard times. Use them to grow and get to know God better.

Do you know that gold is refined and molded through heat? This valuable metal has to go through heat to be transformed into something beautiful. Allow God to heat and mold you through life's tests.

Today's App: What tests are you going through right now? Do you trust your own ability or persevere in the strength of Christ? Ask the Lord to give you the knowledge and eyes to see how He is refining you through difficult trials.

Worrywart

Sarah: "I worry about everything—my friends, my next softball game, and even the geometry test. What can I do?"

God's Text: "You discern my going out and my lying down; you are familiar with all my ways" (Psalm 139:3).

Getting Connected

The definition of "worrywart" is "one who worries excessively and needlessly." Does that describe you? Worrywart is a funny word, but God's Word is clear—worrying is no laughing matter. It can make you physically sick and cause you great stress. Here's the bottom line: When you worry, you aren't trusting God.

King David had lots of things he could have worried about. Whether it was a giant named Goliath, another king who threatened his life, or the people of the nation of Israel he ruled, he had troubles. But David talked to God. Many psalms in the Bible were written by David. They reveal his trust in God. He rested in the fact that God was charting his path and providing for his needs.

When you're tempted to worry, take time to talk to God. Trust that He knows what you're going through and that He has a plan for your life. He can help you be worry free.

Today's App: What giants are you facing today? What circumstances are causing you stress? Remember, God sees you and is with you. If you find yourself worrying, talk to Him and rest in the truth that He is charting your path.

I Feel So Ugly

Callie: "I woke up with a huge zit, and I'm having the worst hair day! I'm feeling ugly."

God's Text: "Charm is deceptive, and beauty is fleeting; but a woman who fears the LORD is to be praised" (Proverbs 31:30).

Getting Connected ●

It's picture day at school. Of all days, you wake up having a bad hair day and a huge zit in the middle of your forehead. What you see in the mirror *is not* what you'd planned as your forever-image in the school yearbook! Most girls have times when they feel ugly, and they always seem to happen on important days. Sometimes feeling pretty seems impossible. The Bible teaches that being beautiful isn't about your outward appearance. God says real beauty shines from the inside. That kind of beauty can only come from the Holy Spirit living within you.

Do you know someone who has a radiance that comes from kindness, humor, gentleness, and generosity? Those qualities really do make a person shine!

Today's App: Are you feeling ugly today? You are God's priceless treasure. He thinks you're beautiful! Adjust your view to match His. And do your actions reflect your inner beauty? Adjust them too if needed.

Inner Beauty

Jennifer: "Did you see Taylor Swift on that awards show? I wish I looked like her."

God's Text: "Your beauty should not come from outward adornment, such as elaborate hairstyles and the wearing of gold jewelry or fine clothes. Rather, it should be that of your inner self, the unfading beauty of a gentle and quiet spirit, which is of great worth in God's sight" (1 Peter 3:3-4).

Getting Connected

Who represents your ideal of beautiful? Taylor Swift has an incredible singing voice, Heidi Klum is a supermodel, and just look at the fame and fortune of Selena Gomez. But what makes them seem beautiful to you? Is it the makeup, the hairstyles, or the gorgeous clothes they wear? What truly makes a woman beautiful? While it's easy to compare yourself to the "beautiful people," that trap will steal your joy and cause you to feel insecure about the beautiful young woman God created *you* to be. In God's sight, your beauty doesn't come from long, flowing hair and pretty clothes. It comes from your heart.

The world doesn't put as much importance on inner beauty, especially because it often isn't noticed at first glance. But as you develop friendships and relationships, remember inner beauty will outlast a new hairstyle or the latest fashion fad.

By the way, the images you see of people don't always reflect the truth. Even supermodels rely on expert makeup and computer software to soften or eliminate wrinkles and blemishes.

Today's App: Do you focus on outer beauty more than inner beauty? How much time do you spend in God's Word each day compared to the time you spend in front of the mirror or in your closet picking out clothes? Real beauty is reflected in your actions and your heart for others.

The Gift of Today

Megan: "Can I be a Christian and still have fun?"

God's Text: "Light in a messenger's eyes brings joy to the heart, and good news gives health to the bones" (Proverbs 15:30).

Getting Connected

Do you sometimes take life too seriously? Do you take risks and reach for the goals you'd like to achieve? God has given you a special gift called *today.* His present to you is *the present.* Jesus came to this world to give you life. He didn't come with a bunch of rules or judgments. He wants you to have an abundant life, a joyful heart, and a future that reflects the wonder, health, and purpose of His best for you.

Don't believe that being a Christian is boring or let anyone trick you into thinking that being a Christian means you don't get to do anything fun. God wants you to experience joy and peace. You have a purpose in life and a future to anticipate! Live one day at a time. Have fun with it. Celebrate Jesus and His gift to you each and every day.

Today's App: Do something fun today—and make sure you give God the glory!

What to Wear

Hayden: "I'm going to the movies, and a guy I like will be there. I have nothing to wear!"

God's Text: "As God's chosen people, holy and dearly loved, clothe yourselves with compassion, kindness, humility, gentleness and patience. Bear with each other and forgive one another if any of you has a grievance against someone. Forgive as the Lord forgave you. And over all these virtues put on love, which binds them all together in perfect unity" (Colossians 3:12-14).

Getting Connected

So, you're going to a movie tonight with your friends, and a guy you like will be there. "What are you going to wear?" That seems like a very important question. Looking good and feeling beautiful is important to girls. A great outfit inspires a bit of courage and confidence, that's true. But a great heart and strong faith creates beauty and inspires confidence from the inside out. And that beauty doesn't change whether you're wearing last year's skirt or this year's favorite accessory.

Do your friends see you as a compassionate and kind young woman? Are you gentle with people? Do you display patience with others? Are you humble? It is okay to desire to look your best outwardly, but the clothing of righteousness is much more fashionable and beautiful to God. And what is beautiful to Him radiates to the people around you.

Today's App: Read again God's text to you. Are you lacking any of the characteristics mentioned? If so, what steps are you going to take to acquire them? Are you "putting on" love? Today's challenge: Clothe yourself in God's fashion choices.

Ordinary Women, Extraordinary Opportunity

Morgan: "I'm just a nobody. Why would God ever choose to use me?"

God's Text: "'I know the plans I have for you,' declares the LORD, 'plans to prosper you and not to harm you, plans to give you hope and a future'" (Jeremiah 29:11).

Getting Connected

You've heard it before, but it's worth hearing again: *God has a plan for your life!* It doesn't matter who you are or what you have done, God can use you to do something great for His glory. Think about the 12 disciples. They weren't necessarily what we would call the elite of society. Even if your past is less than stellar, God will use you if you are willing and available. He doesn't need your ability; He needs your *availability*.

The first chapter of Matthew focuses on the genealogy of Jesus. There are 45 names in the list. Forty of them are men, and five of them are women. The names of the women in the lineage of Jesus are Tamar, Rahab, Ruth, Bathsheba, and Mary. These women were teenagers when God chose to use them. They may have been your age! By *human* standards, each of them had a dark past. Between the five of them, there was rape, adultery, murder, prostitution, and pregnancy out of wedlock. Yet God chose these women because they were available and willing to allow Him free rein. God can use you too, no matter what you have done or experienced. All you have to do is be willing and ready!

Today's App: Do you feel inadequate? Think about the five women in the linage of Jesus. God loved them and used them to fulfill His plans. He can and will use you too if you'll let Him. Say yes to God! Even though you don't know exactly what He will do, you can be assured that you will benefit greatly. He loves you!

The Race You Run

Suzanne: "I hate my outfit. I hate the way I look. My nose is too big, and I feel fat. Why do all my friends look perfect and get all the attention from the guys?"

God's Text: "We do not dare to classify or compare ourselves with some who commend themselves. When they measure themselves by themselves and compare themselves with themselves, they are not wise. We, however, will not boast beyond proper limits, but will confine our boasting to the sphere of service God himself has assigned to us, a sphere that also includes you" (2 Corinthians 10:12-13).

Getting Connected •

Let's face it. Girls can be competitive. Have you noticed the strong desire to completely pick apart your friends or yourself? Why do you bash others and even yourself? You've heard the comments: "I'm not skinny enough." "I'm too skinny so I have no curves." "Her parents give her everything she wants." "I wish my parents made more money." Your words can spread like wildfire, consuming every positive thought if you're not careful.

What race are you running? Are you running a race of competition and comparison? Or are you running a race based on seeking *God's desire* for your life? Are you satisfied with how God made you? Are you content with what you have? Work on boasting in who God is and what He can do through you.

Today's App: Pray for the desire to quit comparing yourself to others or wishing you had something bigger or greater in your life. Open your eyes to everything God blesses you with instead of focusing on what you don't have.

Secret Struggles

Eden: "Lately, I've been cutting myself. My friend says she's going to tell my mom, but I think I have her convinced I've quit. It's my body, why can't I do what I want with it?"

God's Text: "Do not be wise in your own eyes; fear the LORD and shun evil. This will bring health to your body and nourishment to your bones" (Proverbs 3:7-8).

Getting Connected

Everyone has struggles; no one is perfect. For some girls, the struggles seem more intense. They may resort to coping strategies that are unhealthy and unsafe.

Do you know someone who is struggling big time? Are you struggling? If so, don't be afraid to seek help immediately. Draw on the wisdom of Ecclesiastes 4:9-10: "Two are better than one, because they have a good return for their labor: If either of them falls down, one can help the other up. But pity anyone who falls and has no one to help them up."

It might feel difficult to share your struggle with someone. Find the right person to confide in. Remember God is faithful, and He is waiting to help you. You are precious to Him.

Today's App: Praying this prayer will be a good start to seeking help for your struggle:

> *Lord, I'm scared to share this secret. Please give me courage to take the first step. Heal my brokenness and remind me to turn to You when I'm stressed. Guide me to someone who will help me with wisdom based on Your Word. In Your name I pray. Amen.*

The "B" Word

Erika: "I have fallen so far away from God. There is no way He still loves me."

God's Text: "This is what the LORD says to Israel: 'Seek me and live'" (Amos 5:4).

Getting Connected

Do you know the "B" word? *Backslide.* It means that at one time you were moving forward in your journey with the Lord, but now you've started to fall behind. Maybe at one time you were nurturing your relationship with God. Now you feel apathetic about having a quiet time. At one time you were reaching out to others about God, but now it's easier to miss church and not be accountable to your Christian friends or others who might encourage your faith.

Unfortunately, most of us have been there. But we didn't stay there, and you don't have to either. If backsliding describes you, then recognize that the Holy Spirit is nudging you to confess your sin and turn back to living for the Lord. First John 1:9 says, "If we confess our sins, he is faithful and just and will forgive us our sins and purify us from all unrighteousness." Talk to God. He will forgive you, and you can get back on track with Him.

Today's App: Where are you in your walk with the Lord? Are you moving forward or backward? Evaluate where you are and where you need to be. Ask the Lord to help you keep moving ahead and growing closer to Him.

Backseat Drivers

Laura: "I'm just too busy. I don't have any time to help someone today. I don't have time for anything."

God's Text: "I love those who love me, and those who seek me find me" (Proverbs 8:17).

Getting Connected

Being busy is not a sin. Jesus was busy. The disciples were busy. Nothing of importance is achieved without effort and hard work. But being busy in an endless pursuit of the things of this world, such as popularity, money, and possessions, will leave you empty and broken inside. That cannot be pleasing to God.

Often, in the midst of a busy life, the faster you go, the emptier you feel. Take time today to reflect on this question: "Is my drive for worldly things overriding my desire for godly pursuits?" If the answer is yes, you may have to make some hard decisions to bring your life under control and refocus your priorities. Focus on the Father and let everything else take a backseat.

Today's App: Why not pray this today?

Father, help me hear Your voice clearly today. Give me the insight and courage to say no to the world and yes to You. Help me follow You. In Jesus' name. Amen.

Abundant Life

Bobbie: "I feel defeated today. I got a bad grade on a test, and I don't think my friends like me anymore. Where is the joy?"

God's Text: "I am the gate; whoever enters through me will be saved. They will come in and go out, and find pasture. The thief comes only to steal and kill and destroy; I have come that they may have life, and have it to the full" (John 10:9-10).

Getting Connected

How many times do your troubles and hardships make you feel hopeless? Not only is it a bummer to feel so down and out, but there is another problem that comes with so much anguish: faulty thinking. We start buying into the lie that there is nothing better for us and that our situation will never change. But there's good news! Disappointment *does not* have to lead to defeat.

Look closer at what Jesus said in today's promise: "The thief comes only to steal and kill and destroy; I have come that they may have life, and have it to the full." Jesus is sounding the alarm that there will be tough days. Don't take His warning lightly. There is a thief standing by, ready to steal your joy if you are not careful. Praise God that He doesn't leave you there! The promise for you as a believer in Christ is not only eternal life, but life to the *fullest—abundant life!* He wants you to trust His Word and not your feelings when trouble comes.

Today's App: Don't get caught up in faulty thinking that things are hopeless. Enter the gates Jesus Christ has opened for your life. Walk in His truth. Remembering when He has been faithful in the past will help see you through the tough days.

Perfect Love Praying

Carrie Ann: "I can't sleep. I'm scared someone will break in. I don't like being in the dark. What can take away my fear?"

God's Text: "There is no fear in love; but perfect love casts out fear" (1 John 4:18 NASB).

Getting Connected

Fear arrives in many different forms, and it seems to always have bad timing. Have you ever noticed when you're most afraid? Maybe it's when you are around a lot of people. Maybe fear follows you into the classroom right before a test. One thing is certain, fear does not discriminate. At some point, everyone is fearful about something. Nighttime seems like an open invitation for fear to come calling. When it's dark and you're trying to go to sleep, fear can make your imagination run wild.

The problem is you can't just choose for fear to go away. You have to replace that fear with something else. God's Word shows you what to do. Look closely at the words of 1 John 4:18: "There is no fear in love; but perfect love casts out fear." Did you catch the answer to fear? Perfect love. *God* is perfect love! Try some "perfect love praying" next time you are afraid. Tell the Lord your fears. Ask Him to remind you of the truths in His Word. Say out loud the name of your Savior—Jesus!—and watch the perfect Peacemaker change your reaction to the situation.

Today's App: Fear can be paralyzing. Next time you are frozen in fear, remember 1 John 4:18. Perfect love casts out fear. Praying to God and accepting His perfect love takes the place of the fear in your heart and mind. Talk to God about being afraid and watch His power work in your life in a new way.

Gratefulness

Dru: "Everything in life stinks right now. Why isn't anything going right?"

God's Text: "Rejoice always, pray continually, give thanks in all circumstances; for this is God's will for you in Christ Jesus" (1 Thessalonians 5:16-18).

Getting Connected ●

Have you ever watched the television program *Extreme Home Makeover?* Week after week the show focuses on families who are in major need of a better place to live. Even more amazing than the new and beautiful homes constructed are the beautiful attitudes of the families chosen. Most are living in desperate conditions, yet they seem to have one thing in common: gratefulness. Even prior to receiving a new home, most are giving from what little they have to help meet the needs of someone else.

Do you tend to have a pity party mentality? Do you wonder "Why me?" So many times it's easier to focus on what you don't have or what isn't happening than to recognize the ways God is blessing your life. You need to trust in God's plan. Continually remind yourself of all the ways God is blessing you. Remember to be thankful in all circumstances—even when you're having a crummy day.

Today's App: Be joyful, pray continually, and give thanks in all circumstances. Remember, this is God's will for you today. Trust in the Lord's plan and not your own timing and wishes. Check to see if you need a gratitude adjustment.

Choices Matter

Leah: "My friends are going to see a movie tonight. It's rated "R." Should I go?"

God's Text: "Your eye is the lamp of your body. When your eyes are healthy, your whole body also is full of light. But when they are unhealthy, your body also is full of darkness" (Luke 11:34).

Getting Connected ●

Do you ever get tired of all the choices you have to make in one day? Do some decisions seem pretty minor, such as whether you should go see a certain movie? No matter how small the choice, it can have a big effect on your walk with Christ. Whether it's seeing an R-rated movie, listening to songs that have a few cuss words, or peeking at questionable websites, your choices really do matter.

God's Word teaches that what your eyes see directly affects your body. This goes for watching things you know are inappropriate. These impressions don't go away. They slowly dim God's light inside you, eventually turning that bright light into darkness. That's why God's Word stresses how dangerous this can be to your whole body. Have you ever tried to find something in the dark? You stumble, fumble, and end up hurt and lost. Turn on God's light and let Him help you stay on the right path.

Today's App: This week think about what you listen to and what your eyes see. Ask God to show you if they are "light" or "dark" images. One look may not change you immediately, but it leaves its mark. And if you continue in the dark, it will change you forever.

Fun-house Mirror

Deidre: "When I look in the mirror, I see a fat girl with ugly hair and a bad complexion. Why did God make me this way?"

God's Text: "Where can I go from your Spirit [O LORD]...For you created my inmost being; you knit me together in my mother's womb. I praise you because I am fearfully and wonderfully made; your works are wonderful, I know that full well" (Psalm 139:7,13-14).

Get Connected

When you look in the mirror, do you glare at the things you don't like about yourself? When it comes to looks, girls can be their worst critics. When you look closely at your reflection do you cringe and think, "I need to lose five pounds!" or "I need better clothes." Do you panic when you realize you have blemishes on your face? It seems strange, but on the days when you look in the mirror and see the worst, often that's when your friends think you look great. So whose vision is distorted—yours or your friends'? Remember, you both are looking at the same person.

Think of it like looking into a fun-house mirror at a carnival. You tend to see yourself in the worst possible way, when in reality no one else is noticing the flaws or magnifying the features you don't like. Be mindful that when you see a flawed person in the mirror, God sees a special, one-of-a-kind person He created. The psalmist in today's text from God wrote, "[LORD,] your works are wonderful, I know that full well." We know that God's handiwork is beautiful. Don't forget that you are God's handiwork just like the sun, moon, and stars. Why criticize His work in you? Instead of looking into the fun-house mirror image, choose to see yourself in and through God's eyes!

Today's App: Do you get caught up criticizing what you look like? Ask God to free you from the bondage of negative body image and show you how to be happy with who you are. God made you beautiful and unique. No one else is like you.

Sex and Lies

Alyssa: "My body belongs to me. Why do you care what I choose to do with it?"

God's Text: "Do you not know that your bodies are temples of the Holy Spirit, who is in you, whom you have received from God? You are not your own; you were bought at a price. Therefore honor God with your bodies" (1 Corinthians 6:19-20).

Getting Connected •

Everywhere you look sex is there. The ad makers know sex sells, and that's why images about sex show up in what you see and hear. How do you go about keeping your eyes, ears, and heart pure despite the images all around you? One thing is certain, when people operate outside of God's plan, it never makes life better!

Why do you think God commands you to keep pure until you get married? Do you know He covers that in the Bible? Through Paul, God said that people had given in to the sexual desires of their hearts and traded the truth of God for a lie. Because of that lie, they became (are you ready for this?) "filled with every kind of wickedness, evil, greed and depravity. They are full of envy, murder, strife, deceit and malice. They are gossips, slanderers, God-haters, insolent, arrogant and boastful; they invent ways of doing evil; they disobey their parents; they have no understanding, no fidelity, no love, and no mercy" (Romans 1:29-31). Ouch!

God does not want those adjectives to describe you. He wants you to avoid sexual immorality. Sex between a married couple is the ultimate expression of intimacy, and waiting for it should be taken seriously. God doesn't put restrictions on sexual activity to test you or as punishment. He intended sex to be a beautiful expression of love between husband and wife. Abstinence is not a punishment but a protection from physical and emotional dangers.

Today's App: What are some of the lies the enemy promotes about sex? How does God want you to view sex? Is your conduct toward and with boys pleasing to God?

Gripes, Moans, Grumbles

Kara: "I can't believe she did that to me! Who does she think she is?"

God's Text: "Do not judge, and you will not be judged. Do not condemn, and you will not be condemned. Forgive, and you will be forgiven" (Luke 6:37).

Getting Connected

You've probably heard, "If you can't say anything nice, don't say anything at all." Being totally honest, it is almost impossible to go a full day without complaining about something or someone. So, what's a girl to do? Philippians 2:14-15 says, "Do everything without grumbling or arguing, so that you may become blameless and pure, children of God without fault in a warped and crooked generation."

God considers complaining a sin because it breeds ungratefulness. It focuses on what you don't have or don't like rather than what you do have and what you can appreciate. Saying something negative is always regretful because you can never take it back. Once something is spoken, it's out there forever.

When people have hurt you, irritated you, or disappointed you, instead of getting upset, focus on giving them grace and forgiving them when needed. And remember, there have probably been many times when you've needed them to do the same for you.

No one wants to be known for griping, moaning, and grumbling. Stay positive and reflect God's love, grace, and mercy to those around you.

Today's App: Make a list of all the people and things you are grateful for. Now, take a good look at that list. Why waste another drop of energy on complaining? God loves you! He wants to add to your gratitude list.

Measuring Motives

Bethany: "On the outside, people think I'm the perfect Christian. But I'm not perfect. What do I do about the times I do things to please others or make myself look good?"

God's Text: "Be careful not to practice your righteousness in front of others to be seen by them. If you do, you will have no reward from your Father in heaven" (Matthew 6:1).

Getting Connected

Approval and praise can be addictive. When other people single you out because you did something special, does it inflate your ego? If your motive for doing good deeds is to make yourself look good, you may need a reality check.

The Pharisees were especially skilled in following the laws of the land. They prided themselves on doing everything to the letter of the law. Jesus criticized their actions because He knew the motives behind them. Jesus said, "Woe to you, teachers of the law and Pharisees, you hypocrites! You are like whitewashed tombs, which look beautiful on the outside but on the inside are full of the bones of the dead and everything unclean" (Matthew 23:27). He even called them blind fools! All their meticulous efforts to obey God's laws were not rewarded because their motives were self-centered. What seemed like "right living" was steeped more in impressing people.

Today's App: How about you? Evaluate your motives for doing things. Do you crave the approval or praise of others? Do you do things to make yourself look good or because you want to honor God? Ask God to help you have motives that are pure and to do His will whether people are watching or not.

True Character

Natasha: "I feel a lot of pressure to shop at certain stores because the kids at my school make fun of people who don't wear name-brand clothing. What can I do?"

God's Text: "The LORD said to Samuel, 'Do not consider his appearance or his height, for I have rejected him. The LORD does not look at the things people look at. People look at the outward appearance, but the LORD looks at the heart'" (1 Samuel 16:7).

Getting Connected

In a world consumed with red-carpet designs, fashion magazines, and unrealistic "reality" shows, our lust for image has gotten off balance. Even for Christians it's hard not to conform or want to conform. But remember that who you are is not what you look like on the outside. It's who you are underneath your skin. Someone once said that character is a lot like underwear. You can't always see it, but you hope everyone has it!

It's not wrong to want to look attractive, but we become shallow when we place more emphasis on external appearance than character. The apostle Paul shares some fashion tips on our spiritual wardrobe: "As God's chosen people, holy and dearly loved, clothe yourselves with compassion, kindness, humility, gentleness and patience" (Colossians 3:12). These are the things that never go out of style.

Today's App: Your real image is who you are on the inside. Don't be afraid to show your true character. What can you do today to reveal the character of Christ? Praise the achievements of others or do someone a favor. Humility, compassion, and genuine concern for others never go out of style. When you model the character of Christ to others, people will like you for who you are, not who you dress to be.

A Cheerful Giver

Ali: "Why should I give? I'm just a teenager…"

God's Text: "Give, and it will be given to you. A good measure, pressed down, shaken together and running over, will be poured into your lap. For with the measure you use, it will be measured to you" (Luke 6:38).

Getting Connected

The idea of giving your time, your money, or your talents might be hard to grasp and even harder to follow through on. Have you noticed that when you hold tightly to your belongings and blessings with both hands you have no hand open to receive more gifts from God?

The first step in developing a giving mentality is to understand that everything you have comes from God. Your possessions are His, but He lets you hold on to them. Your time here on earth is His, but He lets you use that time. God is gracious to give to you. In return, He asks you to honor Him with the gifts He's given you.

In the Gospel of Luke, the wealthy were giving an offering to God. There was someone else giving that day—a widow. Her offering showed a heart of sacrifice to God because she gave her last two coins (Luke 21). You may feel like you have nothing to give, but it was the widow's small gift that Jesus saw as truly meaningful. "Truly I tell you," Jesus said, "this poor widow has put in more than all the others. All these people gave their gifts out of their wealth; but she out of her poverty put in all she had to live on" (verses 3-4).

Giving isn't about how big the gift is. It's about the heart of the giver. Even if the only thing you have to give is two copper coins, God sees and will be pleased.

Today's App: When was the last time you sacrificed something you really wanted so you could give back to God? God has given you so much to be grateful for! The best response is to give back to Him what was His in the first place. Pray that God will show you how you can give to Him—whether it's through your time, talents, or treasures. You can't out-give God!

Show Me Your Tongue

Destiny: "Nothing ever goes my way. I make plans, but something always seems to go wrong. Why?"

God's Text: "When we put bits into the mouths of horses to make them obey us, we can turn the whole animal. Or take ships as an example. Although they are so large and are driven by strong winds, they are steered by a very small rudder wherever the pilot wants to go. Likewise, the tongue is a small part of the body, but it makes great boasts. Consider what a great forest is set on fire by a small spark" (James 3:3-5).

Getting Connected ●

When you go to the doctor's office, one of the first things your doctor says is, "Stick out your tongue." Your doctor can tell how healthy you are by looking at your tongue's color and bumps. Likewise, through the words you declare, your tongue shows how healthy you are spiritually. In fact, the Bible says your words have the power to create life or death. You've probably heard the expression "Loose lips sink ships." It almost sounds like today's text from God. Even when your circumstances don't look good, you should be careful what you say. How is your tongue guiding your situation? Remember, what you speak influences and even steers your life.

Today's App: Watch the words you let come out of your mouth. Don't say what you see; say what you *want* to see. As you line up your words with scriptural truth, you will see your circumstances change. Molding your future starts with the tiniest member of your body—your tongue.

Is Being a Christian Boring?

Hannah: "Isn't being a Christian boring? What is there to do if you have to follow rules all the time?"

God's Text: "Rejoice always, pray continually, give thanks in all circumstances; for this is God's will for you in Christ Jesus" (1 Thessalonians 5:16-18).

Getting Connected

Do you have friends who make fun of you because you are a Christian? Maybe you've heard them say they want to live by their own rules, create their own excitement, or be carefree and worry about following God when they get older. The world wants you to think that a relationship with Jesus is boring and filled with "do's and don'ts." If you're a Christian, God's Word is alive and active in you. In fact, Jesus calls Christianity the "abundant life." He said, "The thief comes only to steal and kill and destroy; I have come that they may have life, and have it to the full" (John 10:10). So who are you going to believe? Your friends who say, "I'll do it my way!" or the One who tells you, "I am the way"—and His way leads to abundant life?

Today's App: Is your relationship with Christ active or boring? We know from personal experience that when we think a life of faith is boring, it is most likely because we aren't spending enough time with our Savior who longs to hear from us. Just imagine not talking to your best friend for two weeks. Your life would probably seem dull and lonely. Take some time today and talk to Jesus—the One who loves you. You might be surprised how "not boring" your life becomes!

Thinking, Thinking, Thinking

Callie: "Some of my thoughts would not please God, but I can't seem to control what I think about. I've heard verses that say thinking about something is just as bad as doing that action physically. How do I change my thoughts?"

God's Text: "Whatever is true, whatever is noble, whatever is right, whatever is pure, whatever is lovely, whatever is admirable—if anything is excellent or praiseworthy—think about such things" (Philippians 4:8).

Getting Connected ●

All actions start with a thought. Before you ever speak a word, the idea has to pass through your mind first. Even though your brain weighs about three pounds, it is a powerful force in your life when it comes to mind games. So how can your spirit win the battle over your brain?

Isaiah 55:8 reads, "'My thoughts are not your thoughts, neither are your ways my ways,' declares the LORD." The most efficient tools in fighting immoral thoughts are prayer and memorizing Scripture. When you have scripture verses memorized, such as Philippians 4:8 or Isaiah 55:8, you can replace your thoughts with God's thoughts. Even better, give all of your thoughts to God by having your mind set on Him. God says to take every thought captive (2 Corinthians 10:5). If you are struggling with thoughts of fear, or doubt, or sexual immorality, interrupt them and ask Christ to intervene and take over.

Today's App: Don't grow weary in the battle with your thought life! You are not alone. We all struggle with ideas and thoughts that shouldn't be part of our lives. Don't let Satan make you feel alone today. Talk to Jesus about your struggle. Also seek out a close friend or accountability partner and ask her to pray for you.

Is It Time for Bed Yet?

Angelina: "Why am I so tired all the time? I wish I were motivated to go out, but I just want to sleep because I'm so stressed out."

God's Text: "Let us not become weary in doing good, for at the proper time we will reap a harvest if we do not give up" (Galatians 6:9).

Getting Connected ●

Does the world seem like it's on a fast track? With the internet, a smart phone, and 24/7 cable channels, in an instant you can see what is going on around the world. What about your personal life—is it on a fast track too? Do you find yourself crumpling under the weight of the daily grind? Is there no time for rest? How do you step on the brakes when it seems life is speeding by? God invented rest! He established it on the seventh day. And He created it to be good. If you want to hear from God, He tells you how to do so—by being still (Psalm 46:10). How are you at being still and listening for God's leading? It's tough, right?

The important factor is not to give up. You may be going through a season that feels like too much right now. God will not put more on you than you can bear (1 Corinthians 10:13). Sometimes it is important to say no to certain things so you can open up time for yourself and special communion with God.

Today's App: Jesus said, "Come to me, all you who are weary and burdened, and I will give you rest" (Matthew 11:28). Let your mind dwell on this scripture today. Focus on letting Jesus be your rest. He will be strong for you when you can't be strong for yourself.

Fruit of the Spirit and Spiritual Gifts

Chloe: "All this 'Spirit' and spiritual lingo makes *no* sense. Is it real?"

God's Text: "Every good and perfect gift is from above, coming down from the Father of the heavenly lights, who does not change like shifting shadows" (James 1:17).

Getting Connected ●

To have a balanced diet you need to eat fruit every day. God's Word also talks about having fruit in our spiritual diet. Spiritual fruit are God's characteristics we should express to others. Paul wrote, "The fruit of the Spirit is love, joy, peace, patience, kindness, goodness, faith, gentleness self-control. Against such things there is no law" (Galatians 5:22-23 HCSB).

Spiritual gifts are just that—gifts the Holy Spirit has given to every believer in Christ. God's Word talks about the gifts of wisdom, knowledge, faith, healing, prophecy, speaking in tongues, and interpretation of tongues. It also mentions the gifts of serving, teaching, encouraging, giving, leading, and compassion. Not everyone has the same gifts. Like the parts of the body, believers with different gifts make up the whole. We all need each other. All our gifts are important.

The key is to figure out how to connect the two—spiritual fruit and spiritual gifts. God is forming His character in you (fruit) and is helping you develop an area of service (gifts). In His perfect timing He will use you to accomplish His will in your life and in the lives of others.

Today's App: Is God's fruit in you? Yes! Insert your name before each characteristic. For example: *Chloe* is love, *Chloe* is joy, *Chloe* is peace, *Chloe* is patience. Maybe you need to do a fruit check to see if you need to make some adjustments in your spiritual character.

Miss Invisible

Micah: "I feel so alone. No one at school even knows I exist. Is God really here?"

God's Text: "God so loved the world that he gave his one and only Son, that whoever believes in him shall not perish but have eternal life" (John 3:16).

Getting Connected

Do you ever have those days where you feel like you're invisible? Nobody seems to notice you? Nobody seems to care what you say? You can walk through the hallways of school without a single person saying hi? Don't you just want to yell, "I'm here! Hello!" Know that you are not alone. God is always with you, and He loves you more than you will ever know. In fact, the Bible says God even knows how many hairs are on your head. Who else cares so much and pays such attention to what a gift you are? God loves you just the way you are—His unique, precious, one-of-a-kind girl!

Today's App: The next time you feel invisible, pray. Remember, you are loved.

Keep on Keepin' On

Tara: "Why am I such a failure? I seem to fail much more than I succeed! How can a girl start winning in life?"

God's Text: "We are more than *conquerors* through him who loved us" (Romans 8:37).

Getting Connected ●

No one wants to face failures. The joy and wonder is that God does not give up on you—ever! And He doesn't want you to give up on Him either. He keeps working with you to teach you about His power, His faithfulness, and His everlasting love. Believe it or not, He works through your failures more than your successes because then you are usually ready to listen to His wisdom and guidance. Your times of trouble are opportunities for God to reveal His strength to you.

Praise God that the Bible is full of failures who became champions of the faith: Peter, David, Moses, and Jonah just to name a few. Their stories will remind you that your failures can be used for His glory.

Today's text from God provides security. So know that even in failing, you are winning when God is on your side!

Today's App: Paul wrote, "Not that I have already obtained all this, or have already arrived at my goal, but I press on to take hold of that for which Christ Jesus took hold of me" (Philippians 3:12). So keep on keepin' on!

Tempted or Trusting?

Aimee: "My friends smoke so I tried it today. What's the big deal?"

God's Text: "'I have the right to do anything,' you say—but not everything is beneficial. 'I have the right to do anything'—but I will not be mastered by anything" (1 Corinthians 6:12).

Getting Connected

God's desire is for you to pursue holiness because He is holy (1 Peter 1:15). Webster's dictionary defines "holy" as "exalted or worthy of complete devotion as one perfect in goodness and righteousness." The great thing about following the Holy One is the freedom He gives. Freedom in Christ is not just being able to do what you want to do, but also having the power and desire to do what is right.

In a short time, unhealthy actions, including smoking, easily become addictive and very hard habits to break. People have a tendency to become slaves to bad habits. We try to hide the bad habits, and that sends us to a place of shame, loneliness, and despair. God's Word calls our bodies temples of the Holy Spirit (1 Corinthians 6:19). Paul tells us plainly, "Do not give the devil a foothold" (Ephesians 4:27).

Give God your concerns and thank Him for the freedom to serve Him totally. Consider the Lord's love for you, and ask His advice. And then follow through!

Today's App: Thank God for the freedom Christ gives you to live in Him. Galatians 5:1 says, "It is for freedom that Christ has set us free. Stand firm, then, and do not let yourselves be burdened again by a yoke of slavery." Why not pray this today?

Lord, I purpose to trust You and You alone. Guide me with Your wisdom and give me Your strength. In Jesus' name. Amen.

Remove the Roof

Mia: "I want to make God first in my life, but with so much on my plate He often comes in last. How can I change that?"

God's Text: "Seek first [God's] kingdom and his righteousness" (Matthew 6:33).

Getting Connected

Does your to-do list get longer the older you get? If you're like most teens, stress is the result of so much going on. School, parents, friends, boyfriends, and perhaps part-time jobs take their toll. And guess what? Life gets more difficult to manage as you get older. With so much crowding in on your plate, it's easy to see how Jesus can get shoved right out of your day.

If you're frustrated that Jesus is last instead of first in your life, maybe you need to remove the roof. Does this sound crazy? That is exactly what four friends did, according to chapter 2 in the Gospel of Mark. The men were desperate to get their paralyzed friend to Jesus. They knew He was the only answer for their hurting friend who needed healing. When they arrived at the home where Jesus was teaching, they couldn't get through the door because of all the people. Something drastic had to happen. So what did they do? They made an opening in the roof above Jesus and lowered their friend down on a mat (verse 4). They removed the obstacle between them and Jesus and placed their friend right in His presence. And when Jesus saw their faith, he told the paralyzed man, "Your sins are forgiven...Get up, take your mat and go home" (verses 5 and 11). Problem solved!

Today's App: When you consider everything on your to-do list, which ones are obstacles to spending time with Jesus? What is crowding Him out? Only you can do the soul searching necessary to know what is hindering your faith. If you need to, be willing to do something drastic to get to Jesus. He is waiting for you.

The Born-again Identity

Alex: "I look at myself in the mirror and see a person unworthy of anyone's love, much less the love of God. What does God see when He looks at me?"

God's Text: "He chose us in him before the creation of the world to be holy and blameless in his sight" (Ephesians 1:4).

"I pray that the eyes of your heart may be enlightened in order that you may know the hope to which [God] has called you" (Ephesians 1:18).

Getting Connected •

Describe yourself in three words. Are your adjectives positive or negative? Girls can be quite critical of themselves. Do you ever ask, "Why don't I measure up?" The world says your identity comes from the things you possess, how much money your family has, what brand of clothes you wear, the neighborhood you live in, what boy you are dating, and what you accomplish. If you fall into the trap of trying to identify yourself by these human standards, you will eventually fall short.

Instead, look to Christ for your identity. What does it mean to have your identity in Christ? It's knowing you are valuable because God loves you. He created you. He watches over you. You are so important to Him that His Son Jesus died so you could know God intimately and for eternity!

If you are a believer, God has given you countless blessings, including salvation, grace, forgiveness, and mercy. You have been given gifts from God that are more important than having millions in the bank or dating the most popular guy in school.

And on the flip side of this great relationship, Christ stands with you. Think about it. When you face a trial, God goes through it with you. *You are never alone.* The Creator of the universe has your back no matter what life throws your way. God's text today says "He chose us." God chose you to be one of His children. Walk in the confidence of that truth instead of believing the world's message about who you are.

Today's App: "See to it that no one takes you captive through hollow and deceptive philosophy, which depends on human tradition and the elemental spiritual forces of this world rather than on Christ" (Colossians 2:8). Ask God to help you find your identity in Him. Choose to walk in the truth that He loves you and has given you immeasurable gifts that the world and its possessions can't compare to.

Got Ya Covered

Monique: "My fashion style is to keep up with the trends. I know some outfits are a little shorter or more revealing than others, but what's the big deal?"

God's Text: "I also want the women to dress modestly, with decency and propriety, adorning themselves, not with elaborate hairstyles or gold or pearls or expensive clothes, but with good deeds, appropriate for women who profess to worship God" (1 Timothy 2:9-10).

Getting Connected ●

Are you a fashionista? When it comes to your personal style, what trend are you following? Being trendy can create trouble. You may be like Monique, who thinks it's no big deal to wear short skirts and tops that are low cut. When you look in a mirror, you're looking at the "big picture"— at all of you. You take in the view all at once, even turning sideways to see how you look from head to toe.

Boys, on the other hand, are different. Did you know they are stimulated by sight? Stimulated means aroused, excited, turned on. So now imagine that same outfit you want to wear from a guy's perspective. A short skirt lures a boy's eyes straight to your legs. And what about that low-cut top? A guy is probably no longer looking at your eyes. The way you dress is a big deal because it can be a distraction from the real you.

God's Word holds the key to your closet. Today's text from God talks about dressing modestly and decently. Think of it as God looking out for your best interests. You can still look cute—just do a final check to make sure your clothing choices have you covered.

Today's App: Do you need a dressing do over? Keep modesty in mind when you're choosing clothes for the day. Don't get caught on *God's* camera for the TV show *What Not to Wear*.

Duct Tape Your Thoughts

Corbin: "I have a problem of blurting out what I'm thinking. How can I tame my tongue?"

God's Text: "Do not let any unwholesome talk come out of your mouths, but only what is helpful for building others up according to their needs, that it may benefit those who listen" (Ephesians 4:29).

Getting Connected

People can be so creative. Have you noticed the many things that can be done with duct tape? Some of the most elaborate prom dresses have been made with duct tape. Google it sometime. People laugh while saying that the only way to keep someone from getting in trouble with her mouth is to tape it shut. Maybe not a bad idea, especially if you are the one who has regretted something you've said.

So how do you cover your thoughts without using tape so you won't blurt something out? Try repeating these lines: "Think it, speak it… unwise." Now add these words, "Think it, restrain it…wise." Say it again out loud: "Think it, speak it…unwise. Think it, restrain it…wise."

God's Word tells us our talk should be wholesome so "it may benefit those who listen." Remember your words and tone of voice can carry a lot of volume, and more people may be tuning in than you realize.

Today's App: Practice makes perfect. Repeat this line over and over today: "Think it, speak it…unwise. Think it, restrain it…wise."

Showers of Mercy

Rachelle: "Every day I wake up praying that I will get it right and not mess up, but every day I always fall short. Can you help?"

God's Text: "Because of the LORD's faithful love we do not perish, for His mercies never end. They are new every morning; great is Your faithfulness!" (Lamentations 3:22-23 HCSB).

Getting Connected ●

When you were a little girl, did you write on your driveway or the sidewalk with chalk? Maybe you drew flowers or wrote your name. Your parents thought it was a mess, but there on the concrete was your wonderful masterpiece. Then a rainstorm or the water sprinkler washed it away before everyone could admire it. Showers of water wash away chalk on a sidewalk just like showers of mercy from God wash away your mistakes and mess-ups.

As a Christian, you are not called to perfection. You are called to *follow* the One who is perfect. Every day you will mess up. It never fails. It is human nature to sin. Jesus said, "Whoever wants to be my disciple must deny themselves and take up their cross daily and follow me" (Luke 9:23). Jesus made a point to say *daily*. Each day, you have to make a conscious, deliberate decision to follow Christ. Every day you mess up, and every day you get another chance to get it right. God knew you would continually mess up—that's why He gives you His mercy. God doesn't look at you and see all of the mishaps of yesterday. No, He sees a blank slate, a fresh start, made clean by His showers of love.

Today's App: Make a conscious effort to take time every morning to commit your day to the Lord. Don't fall into the trap of believing that following Him is a one-time commitment. Ask God to show you how to be more dedicated in serving Him.

Is Thin Really In?

Carson: "All my friends are so skinny. Some girls say I should quit eating. Others say to go ahead and eat but throw up right afterward. I want to fit in with my group and into my jeans, but these ideas seem really weird."

God's Text: "The mind governed by the flesh is death, but the mind governed by the Spirit is life and peace" (Romans 8:6).

Getting Connected

Did you hear it? That gentle whisper inside, alerting you that something isn't right? Just like Carson, something seemed off when her friends started talking about throwing up to lose weight. If your spirit even feels a little weird about an activity, run away! The Lord whispers inside you so you will know when you are playing with fire (1 Kings 19:11-13).

God's Word says the flesh is a dangerous thing. But when your mind is ruled by His Spirit, something divine happens. Christ gives you life in abundance and peace. The Bible is absolute in letting you know that you are His. Your identity in Him is not dependent on how others see you or even how you see yourself. What's even more beautiful is that your eternity is based on the fact that God sees you as righteous through Christ! Fitting into God's plan for you is the best feeling you'll ever have.

Today's App: Seeing yourself as acceptable...fine. Jesus seeing you as perfect... priceless!

I Can

Brooke: "Sometimes I feel like my friends don't like me because I'm better than them at basketball. What should I do?"

God's Text: "We are God's handiwork, created in Christ Jesus to do good works, which God prepared in advance for us to do" (Ephesians 2:10).

Getting Connected ●

If God has given you a certain gift or talent, He did it for a reason! This is where confidence and an "I can" attitude make the difference in how your friends respond to your God-given abilities. Do you know that the commandment repeated most often throughout the Bible is "do not fear"? God talks about it more than He talks about love, which is the greatest commandment!

This indicates how badly God wants you to live "in Him" confidently, not letting fear into your heart. The opposite of being fearful is being brave, which can also be called confident. Anytime you face someone who is criticizing you for doing too good of a job, or the flip side of not being good enough, remember there are hundreds of encouraging words in God's Book to remind you "to not be afraid" of who you are and to do your best with the gifts and talents God has given you.

Whether it is sports, cheerleading, music, or academics, remember, "The LORD himself goes before you and will be with you; he will never leave you nor forsake you. Do not be afraid; do not be discouraged" (Deuteronomy 31:8).

Today's App: You don't always have to *be* the best, but you are always encouraged to *do* your best! Give 100 percent and let God take care of the rest.

RELATIONSHIPS

Do you ever feel like you are on relationship overload? You know...

- other girls
- guys
- all those grown-ups

You are at an age when facing daily drama from other girls can be overwhelming. How do you handle pressure from your friends or your boyfriend, if you have one? What about expectations from your parents and teachers and other adults? The good news is you don't have to figure this out alone. You have help right at your fingertips from the best relationship expert ever. God has the answer to every question you have when it comes to dealing with people. See what His Word says about the relationships in your life. Let Him show you how to turn "overwhelming" into a surplus of "no regret" connections.

Blessings,
Robin

The Need for Mercy

Maggie: "I'm so mad at my friend right now—and it is totally her fault!"

God's Text: "By this everyone will know that you are my disciples, if you love one another" (John 13:35).

Getting Connected

It's easy to become so mad that you want revenge. You'd love to see the person pay for what she did to you. You want to see her be miserable for once. But hold on. Is that what God's Word says to do? While we love to accept God's mercy for the things we've done wrong, sometimes we forget we need to extend His mercy and forgiveness to those who have wronged us.

Showing mercy to others is a *choice*. It may not always be easy. While you may be angry on the inside, giving love and kindness to someone who wronged you is showing the love of Christ. The more you extend mercy to others, the more like Christ you will become. It's better to choose obedience to God's instruction than to follow your sinful desire of payback.

Today's App: Has someone recently hurt you or said something that caused you pain? Realize that because you have the Holy Spirit living inside you, you have the power to offer kindness, mercy, and forgiveness based on God's love. Try it and see what God will do!

Set the Example

Libby: "My friends are going to a party. I want to go so I'll fit in."

God's Text: "In everything set them an example by doing what is good. In your teaching show integrity, seriousness and soundness of speech that cannot be condemned, so that those who oppose you may be ashamed because they have nothing bad to say about us" (Titus 2:7-8).

Getting Connected

It's natural to want to hang out with friends and be accepted by others. But what happens when you are put in a compromising situation? When you are faced with choosing to go with the crowd or to set a godly example? God calls you to be holy—which means being set apart. Your life should be a reflection of biblical values—not the values or priorities of the world. Your actions may look odd to those who don't believe in Christ. Whether it's choosing not to drink or use foul language, your actions will show others a different way of living. The integrity you show through your words, choices, and behavior is part of your testimony of Christ and what He is doing within you and through you.

Today's App: It's okay to be different! Choose to be a godly example for your friends so they'll be encouraged to seek Christ. Yes, you may experience some ridicule, but you'll also gain the respect of many others when you live a life of integrity. You also might be providing support for others in your group who aren't strong enough to take a stand alone.

Action Counts

Brittany: "One of my friends can be so rude it makes me angry. What can I do?"

God's Text: "Blessed are the merciful, for they will be shown mercy" (Matthew 5:7).

Getting Connected

How common is it for you to develop a bad attitude toward someone? Maybe you're irritated with a friend, a parent, or your little brother. Maybe a teacher or someone you don't even know is rubbing you the wrong way. It's easy to complain, but it takes grace to take godly action. God says to have an attitude of mercy. He gives instructions in His Word about maintaining and restoring relationships through grace.

Luke 17:3-4 says, "So watch yourselves. If your brother or sister sins against you, rebuke them; and if they repent, forgive them. Even if they sin against you seven times in a day and seven times come back to you saying "I repent," you must forgive them." To rebuke doesn't mean to point out every sin a person commits, but it means you're to speak truth with gentle love for the purpose of restoring that person to God and to others.

Before you point out sin in someone else's life, pray and confess any sin you may have in your own heart. Jesus took the ultimate action of offering mercy and forgiveness when He died on the cross. What can you do to develop an attitude of mercy and action toward those who've wronged you?

Today's App: Is there someone in your life that needs your mercy? Do you have a bad attitude toward someone who has wronged you? Write that person's name on a notecard and place it where you will see it several times for the next few days. Each time you see that name, ask the Lord to help you extend mercy to him or her.

Finding Friends

Becca: "Why is Paige hanging out with that group of girls? All they do is trash talk other girls—even the ones who are their friends."

God's Text: "Let no one deceive you with empty words, for because of such things God's wrath comes on those who are disobedient. Therefore do not be partners with them" (Ephesians 5:6-7).

Getting Connected •

Face it, girl. In today's culture there's a lot of pressure to find the perfect guy, have the perfect friends, and look like a celebrity at a photo shoot. It's easy to get a skewed vision about what is good and what is not so good. So how do you respond when someone warns you about the friends you've surrounded yourself with? Do you cover your ears?

It's natural to want to believe the best about people, but God's Word reminds you to consistently be on guard in the area of relationships. If someone raises a red flag, even if it's your mom, pray and ask the Lord to help you determine if the relationship will help you grow in your spiritual journey or pull you down. Loving someone and being nice to others is always a good thing, but the people you choose as close friends and as a boyfriend will affect your future.

Today's App: Do you have a gut feeling that suggests you need to be cautious in a particular friendship? Do your friends make you a better person? Don't risk being involved in bad relationships. Be satisfied and secure in the relationship you have with your heavenly Father, and ask Him to give you the strength needed to make the right choices.

Foolish Fighting

Bella: "Sarah was so mean today. She said I couldn't be trusted because I told Molly about the crush she has on Derek. Why is she being so dramatic?"

God's Text: "Like one who grabs a stray dog by the ears is someone who rushes into a quarrel not their own" (Proverbs 26:17).

Getting Connected

Have you been in a situation where you told someone's secret and then got caught? Even though girls are tempted to gossip, the Bible is very specific about how destructive the tongue can be. Ephesians 4:29 says, "Do not let any unwholesome talk come out of your mouths, but only what is helpful for building others up according to their needs, that it may benefit those who listen."

What will you do the next time you're tempted to share someone's secret? First, stop and think *before* you open your mouth. Ask, "Will what I'm about to say benefit my friend or tear her down?" Use self-control. Say only things that build people up or say nothing at all. Dare to be different than the other girls at school. Be a light for Christ in the world.

Today's App: Consider why you talk about others. Ask the Lord to help you stay out of the girl drama that can consume you. Pray this prayer:

Dear Lord, I understand gossip has many negative effects on people's lives. It causes pain and can leave scars on friendships. Help me stay out of conversations that involve hurtful words. Allow me to be an encourager to others. In Your name. Amen.

Mom Again?

Laurel: "My mom is so annoying! She won't let me go out with friends past midnight. We just want to see a movie. What's so wrong about that?"

God's Text: "Do not blaspheme God or curse the ruler of your people" (Exodus 22:28).

Getting Connected ●

Think about a time when your mom really frustrated you. Now ask, "Why did the situation frustrate me so much?" If you're really honest, it probably boiled down to one thing: You didn't get your way. Whatever the situation, the Bible is clear on how you should respond to authorities: with respect.

Now, let's look at it from a different angle. The Bible wants you to obey your parents. But more importantly, you should *want* to treat your parents and other authorities with respect. This is as much about the condition of your heart as it is about the person you are respecting. What's on the inside is revealed by your outward actions. When you disrespect your parents, you are also disrespecting God.

Today's App: Imagine being in a heated debate with your mom. Put yourself in that moment. Now, take a deep breath. Ask God to give you the strength to respond without disrespect and talking back. Remember, your mom has your best interest at heart. Even when it seems she isn't showing you respect, demonstrate the love of Christ. You will definitely be blessed by Him for honoring your mom.

Tongue-tied?

Tiffanie: "I want to tell my friends about God, but I'm not sure I know enough. How will I know what to say?"

God's Text: "I will give you words and wisdom that none of your adversaries will be able to resist or contradict" (Luke 21:15).

Getting Connected

Do you worry that you don't know enough Bible to share your faith? You're not alone. Fear and inadequacy are the top reasons Christians don't share their faith. Did you know Moses feared being tongue-tied and incapable of carrying out God's mission? God assured Moses in the midst of his fear that He was with him. And sure enough, when Moses moved forward in faith, God gave him the words to say.

The same is true for you. If you've hesitated to tell your friends about God, it's okay. But don't let fear stop you from allowing God to use you in someone's life. God promises He will give you the words and the wisdom. Sharing God's message can make an eternal difference in the life of someone today.

Today's App: Remember these three T's: *take* the risk, *talk* about Jesus, and *trust* God will keep you from being tongue-tied.

Parent Trap

Kasey: "My parents don't have a clue. Do I still have to do what they say?"

God's Text: "Honor your father and your mother, so that you may live long in the land the LORD your God is giving you" (Exodus 20:12).

Getting Connected •

Do you ever feel trapped between a rock and hard place when it comes to communicating with your parents? Do you think they just don't understand you or what your life is really like? God has a specific message for you: "Honor your father and your mother." Those words from God are in one of the oldest books of the Bible. The word "honor" is not outdated though. You may not use that word much in your daily life, but you know what it means to honor someone. Dictionary.com defines "honor" as "being respectful," but it also means showing "a courteous regard for."

You don't always have to agree with your parents, but God calls you to *respect* them and be courteous. What does this look like? Well, the next time your mom asks you to clean your room, respond promptly and without grumbling. Take a moment to mentally acknowledge that your parents provide for you, and you should respect the room they make possible. When your dad asks you to come home at a certain time, respect his desire so he doesn't worry. God doesn't give the command to honor your parents to make your life harder. He wants what's best for you, and often what is best is what happens when you honor your parents.

Today's App: The next time you find yourself butting heads with your parents, remember to be respectful and courteous.

Mentor Wanted

Morgan: "I need someone to confide in. Jessica says I should talk to my mom, but I'm not sure I want her to know my personal thoughts. What do you think?"

God's Text: "Confess your sins to each other and pray for each other so that you may be healed. The prayer of a righteous person is powerful and effective" (James 5:16).

Getting Connected ●

Who do you turn to when you need advice? Why do you talk to that person? Does she have a close relationship with Christ? Who you go to for advice is an incredibly crucial aspect of your walk with God. If you consistently go to someone who is giving you negative feedback or encouraging you to do unhealthy things, you are not getting fed in the way the Holy Spirit longs for you to be.

It's so important to talk to someone you love and trust—your parents, your grandparents, your Sunday school teacher, or a teacher you respect. Even though it might be hard to talk about your feelings and thoughts, wise counsel will help you more than an unhealthy friendship ever could. Be brave and know that God is the ultimate advice giver. He is with you always!

Today's App: Pray that God will put a good mentor in your life who can help disciple you in your relationship with Christ:

> *Dear God, please bring someone into my life I can talk to.*
> *Give me the strength and courage to share even when it's*
> *difficult. Help me know this person loves and cares for me*
> *the way You desire. If I've been getting unhealthy advice,*
> *please remove the lies or unwise leading from my mind and*
> *replace them with Your truths. In Jesus' name. Amen.*

Stamp of Approval

Esther: "Did you see Julia's outfit today? She is so weird. I don't want her to be part of our group anymore."

God's Text: "Accept one another, then, just as Christ accepted you, in order to bring praise to God" (Romans 15:7).

Getting Connected

Do you ever feel like Julia? Like you don't fit in with a certain group or that people keep you on the outside? It's pretty natural to want to be accepted and approved by others. But Paul said, "Am I now trying to win the approval of human beings, or of God? Or am I trying to please people? If I were still trying to please people, I would not be a servant of Christ" (Galatians 1:10).

The great thing is that Christ accepts everyone. No one has to work to win His love or mercy. He offers it to everyone as a gift. You may not always win the approval of other girls. And you shouldn't try to make girls please you. Don't become the girl who tries to change her friend because you don't like the clothes she wears or the music she listens to. Accept her as Christ does.

Today's App: Here's a prayer for today:

Dear God, help me not be so hard on others. Remind me that the most important thing is to know You approve of me. I need Your love, God. Your blessing, acceptance, and unconditional love lead me to happiness and purpose. In Jesus' name. Amen.

Care for the Least of These

Corbin: "I'm really concerned about girls who run away from home and end up on the street. How can I help them?"

God's Text: "If anyone gives even a cup of cold water to one of these little ones who is my disciple, truly I tell you, that person will certainly not lose their reward" (Matthew 10:42).

Getting Connected

Have you ever had one of those "It's all about me" moments? The truth is, we've all had them. Whether it's poverty, sickness, or homelessness, believers have a responsibility to care for those who need help.

If it's not your nature to be burdened for those who are hurting, ask the Lord to give you a special antenna today—one that will pick up on people who could use help. Ask the Holy Spirit to help you offer friendship and kindness to those who are hurting.

Do you have a strong burden for the hurting world? Explore ways you can volunteer. Ask your parents or youth minister to help you find somewhere to serve, perhaps at a local shelter or children's hospital. Consider a career where you can make a difference on a daily basis. You may be the only reflection of God some people ever see.

Today's App: Open your eyes today to see people as God sees them. Ask God to show you where and how you can help someone today.

It's Wise to Witness

Hattie: "I love the Lord so much. But it's hard to talk about Him with others. I'm afraid they'll think I'm strange."

God's Text: "The fruit of the righteous is a tree of life, and the one who is wise saves lives" (Proverbs 11:30).

Getting Connected

Whether you are the captain of a sports team, involved in choir, participate in a class project, or are just doing your thing, people are watching you. Every day, by example or by words, you can lead others to consider a relationship with the Lord. People need Jesus and His saving grace. You can give them hope for the forgiveness of their sins and a future life in eternity by showing them who Jesus is. Can anything be more important?

Put aside your feelings of inadequacy and any fear you might have. Pursue saving someone's life by introducing them to Christ! Not everyone will listen, but don't stop sharing. Ask Jesus to empower you through His Holy Spirit, who lives within you.

Today's App: "I can do all things through [Christ] who strengthens me" (Philippians 4:13 NASB). Pray for an opportunity to share the gift of faith!

Lord, bring someone across my path today and open a way to testify about Your wonders and grace. In Your name. Amen.

Sharing Means Caring

Jackie: "I'm worried about my friend Cindy. She is so down and struggles with her less-than-ideal home life. I want to help her, but I don't know how."

God's Text: "We ought always to thank God for you, brothers and sisters, and rightly so, because your faith is growing more and more, and the love all of you have for one another is increasing" (2 Thessalonians 1:3).

Getting Connected

Do you have friends who are sad, troubled, neglected, or ignored? You have the answer—Jesus Christ! You know the answer and yet you hesitate to bring it out in the open. What are you afraid of? Embarrassment? Lack of knowledge of God's Word? Rejection? Proverbs 3:5 says, "Trust in the LORD with all your heart and lean not on your own understanding." Step out boldly and tell your friends, family, and others about the Good News of Jesus Christ!

Let the Spirit of God work through you to reach others for Him. On the basis of what God's Word says—that God cannot lie and you will not be disappointed if you hope in Him—share Jesus with everyone you meet. Help people go from stumbling to standing tall.

Today's App: "Faith comes from hearing the message, and the message is heard through the word about Christ" (Romans 10:17). Pay attention to God's Word. Listen to it. Read it. Memorize it. And share it with others.

Forgive the Hurt

Carissa: "Natalie has told so many lies about me. Forgiving is hard enough, but do I really have to forget?"

God's Text: "Smart people know how to hold their tongue; their grandeur is to forgive and forget" (Proverbs 19:11 MSG).

Getting Connected

After being sold into slavery by his jealous brothers and being falsely accused of rape and thrown into prison, Joseph had every reason to be angry and bitter. In a gripping encounter with his brothers 13 years later, Joseph said: "You intended to harm me, but God intended it for good to accomplish what is now being done, the saving of many lives" (Genesis 50:20). Wow! That's God's grace and healing in action.

We don't know how long it took Joseph to get to the point of forgiveness. Since he grew up as his father's favorite child, he must have battled a pretty bad case of TPS—teacher's pet syndrome—along with its common symptoms of pride and blaming others. Even though Joseph knew his brothers originally planned to murder him, somewhere along the line Joseph chose to forgive and forget. Forgiveness freed him from the bondage of anger and resentment.

Today's App: Even if you have every reason to be angry, don't sacrifice all you can accomplish in God's strength by wasting time and energy in a prison of bitterness. Choose to forgive and forget and trust God to redeem the situation and give you peace.

Choose Friends Carefully

Sierra: "Amanda used to be my best friend, but lately she has become so disrespectful. She argues with her mom about every little thing and even talks bad about her other friends. Should I keep hanging out with her?"

God's Text: "Walk with the wise and become wise, for a companion of fools suffers harm" (Proverbs 13:20).

Getting Connected

People will judge you by the people you hang out with. What's worse is that the Bible says you'll eventually learn their ways. "Do not be misled: 'Bad company corrupts good character'" (1 Corinthians 15:33). In other words, show me your friends and I can likely guess your moral character and predict some of your future goals.

Just like your cell phone can suggest the words you want to use in text messages, the friends you hang out with can predict and fill in the path of decisions you'll make toward your future. So pick your friends carefully. They not only influence who you become, but they also help shape your destiny. A great aspect of this wisdom is that *you* can be a good influence in your group as you walk in God's truth and become one of the "wise" ones. As you do this, you'll attract and be attracted to like-minded, like-hearted friends.

Today's App: Make a list of goals that are important to you, such as having good relationships with family members, developing your spiritual life, and doing well in school. If your current friends don't value the same goals, pursue relationships with people who do. Look for godly friendships that will challenge you to live like Christ.

Mean Girls

Hannah: "The girls at school are so mean to me. I 'turn the other cheek,' but I know they are gossiping and telling secrets about me that aren't true. I've had enough! I want to do the same thing to them! How do I stay on the right path?"

God's Text: "Do not take revenge, my dear friends, but leave room for God's wrath, for it is written: 'It is mine to avenge; I will repay,' says the Lord" (Romans 12:19).

Getting Connected

There will always be the mean girls. They are unavoidable. Somehow they find a way to really get under your skin. Girls can be nice to your face but then say something mean as soon as you walk away. Even women gossip and hurt each other's feelings. You can't always count on a mean girl growing out of her attitude.

It's important to learn how to handle mean girls so that they don't impact you negatively and bring you down to their level. The secret to dealing with troublemakers is to trust that God will take care of you and use this struggle to make your walk with Him stronger.

What can you do when you are hurt? It's okay to cry and mourn the hurt. In fact, the deeper you cry out to God, the deeper He can heal you. And remember, mean girls have to lay their heads down on their pillows at night knowing how they acted that day. Ask the Lord to bring you supportive friends. Journal your prayers so you have visible reminders of how God helps you.

Today's App: Even though it's hard to understand why girls can be so mean, it's important to realize you don't know what their home lives are like or what hurts they might be hiding behind their behavior. There is no excuse for people to be mean, but instead of retaliating with anger, pray for them. Ask God to help you be His witness to that person. Remember that God is always in control, and He will most assuredly take care of you.

Kindness Kills Offense

Jessie: "I can't stand the way Emily looks at me. Every time I'm around her my skin crawls. It's like she thinks she's better than me."

God's Text: "A person's wisdom yields patience; it is to one's glory to overlook an offense" (Proverbs 19:11).

Getting Connected •

It's human nature to want to react and attack when other girls say or do things that hurt you. Retaliating, however, only reinforces the vicious cycle of hurt. Hurting people hurt others. Where does the circle of pain end? It *can* stop with you. When someone offends you, does your mind magnify the circumstance until it's blown way out of proportion? If a person hurts your pride or feelings, your response can turn the offense into a deep wound. Not every injustice is a matter of right or wrong. Sometimes God is trying to develop the fruit of forgiveness in you. If you are never offended, you will never have the opportunity to forgive.

Overlooking an offense is a choice. It's not something you do just for the other person. It's something you do out of obedience to God. It also purifies you from the toxicity of bitterness and produces the fruit of forgiveness in you.

Today's App: Refuse to allow the bitter disease of offense to grow in you. Take your hurt to God and pray for the other girl. More than likely she has been hurt by someone else. Ask God to bless her and to help you be compassionate toward her. When you see her again, say something nice. Kindness is like disinfectant— it kills offenses on contact.

Worth the Wait

Claire: "I know it's wrong to get sexually involved with a guy, but everyone else is doing it. My friends think my purity stance is hyperspiritual. Is it really worth the wait?"

God's Text: "I press on toward the goal to win the prize for which God has called me heavenward in Christ Jesus" (Philippians 3:14).

Getting Connected

God designed us to have sexual desires, but He also gave us guidelines for handling those desires. Just like a mother instructs her young children not to play in the street because she knows it's dangerous, God knows the dangers of premarital sex. He didn't instruct us to refrain from sex to punish us. He gave us guidelines to protect us and enhance the intimacy we will one day share with our spouses.

Satan wants to spoil that intimacy. He wants to convince you that it's okay to sneak a peek—to tear the packaging on the Christmas present early. He wants to make you think there's no reason to wait. Don't fall for his lies! God doesn't call you to do something that is not for your absolute best. Just like there are costs for compromising on God's values, there are prizes for maintaining purity.

Today's App: A runner doesn't run a race without his eye on the prize. Neither should you lose sight of your goal. There will be opponents who try to steal your place, but don't let them lead you off course. Set boundaries to protect your purity. Keep your eyes fixed on God's principles and ask Him to help you visualize your prize. The rewards are worth the wait.

Little Christ

Stacey: "I found out today that one of my close friends at school is not a Christian. I want to talk to her about God. Where do I start?"

God's Text: "Go and make disciples of all nations, baptizing them in the name of the Father and of the Son and of the Holy Spirit, and teaching them to obey everything I have commanded you. And surely I am with you always, to the very end of the age" (Matthew 28:19-20).

Getting Connected

Did you know the term "Christian" literally means "little Christ"? This is a reminder that as a Christian, you are God's ambassador everywhere you go. "To this you were called, because Christ suffered for you, leaving you an example, that you should follow in his steps" (1 Peter 2:21). Witnessing really is as simple as following Jesus' footprints. He has already paved the way for you. If you are having a hard time finding His path or sharing His path with others, relax and know that God is with you always. He will guide you and encourage you. "Be strong and courageous. Do not be afraid or terrified…the LORD your God goes with you; he will never leave you nor forsake you" (Deuteronomy 31:6). God will be your voice when you are unsure of what to say. You need only to be still and trust that He is in full control of your life. He wants you to succeed!

Today's App: Take the time to listen to God. Let Him direct your thoughts and actions in witnessing. Your actions will speak louder than your words ever will. Pray for your friends and loved ones often. God will open doors for you to share Jesus.

Accountability Partner

Denise: "My youth pastor's message last night was about having an accountability partner. I don't see the point. I don't trust people as it is, so why would I want to tell someone my struggles?"

God's Text: "Two are better than one, because they have a good return for their labor: If either of them falls down, one can help the other up. But pity anyone who falls and has no one to help them up...Though one may be overpowered, two can defend themselves. A cord of three strands is not quickly broken" (Ecclesiastes 4:9-10,12).

Getting Connected

A simple way to explain accountability is "answering for your actions." As a Christian, you are held to a higher accountability in Jesus Christ. That's why it's important to seek a deeper relationship with God and your fellow brothers and sisters in Christ. Is there someone you can talk to one-on-one who will listen to your struggles and victories with love and offer godly wisdom?

Proverbs 27:6 says, "Wounds from a friend can be trusted, but an enemy multiplies kisses." Accountability is not to beat you up but rather to lift you up. Scripture says someone who directs you toward God and encourages you to keep your head up and overcome sin is going to take you a lot further than a friend who leads you astray—away from the presence of God.

Some girls choose one of their parents or siblings to be their accountability partner. For others, it's a close friend, a youth pastor, or female mentor from church. Take into consideration that person's life. Is she trustworthy? Pray for God to direct you to the right person.

Today's App: Ask God to open your eyes to someone you trust who can mentor you. Remember, no one is perfect, and we are here to get through trials and triumphs together. Let someone help you grow closer to God, and in return you can do the same for her.

Guy Guidelines

Taylor: "I have this list of things I can't do with a boy. What exactly *can* I do?"

God's Text: "God did not call us to be impure, but to live a holy life" (1 Thessalonians 4:7).

Getting Connected ●

One teenage daughter asked her mom the very question Taylor is asking. The mom gave her daughter a very practical answer. She said that whatever they did with their dad is pretty much what they can do with their boyfriends. If your dad believes in Jesus and is committed to biblical values, that advice might also be a guideline for you. Would you hold your dad's hand? Would you give him a big hug? Would you kiss him on the cheek? Would you sit with him and laugh so hard you could cry? All of these things are normal, natural, and totally appropriate. Anything beyond those guidelines pushes the limit. Talk to your mom and dad about dating do's and don'ts.

"Don't let anyone look down on you because you are young, but set an example for the believers in speech, in conduct, in love, in faith and in purity" (1 Timothy 4:12). This doesn't have to be a tough task. You can do it! You just have to set your mind on the goal and then surround yourself with friends who will hold you accountable. Be the example God has called you to be!

Today's App: Make a list of friends you trust, and ask them if they would be willing to help you with your purity walk. Consider asking your dad to help you purchase a purity ring or purity necklace. These are great ways to show people you are serious about your commitment to Christ.

Comparison Crisis

Mandy: "Why does everyone else's life seem better than mine?"

God's Text: "Give thanks to the LORD, for he is good; his love endures forever" (1 Chronicles 16:34).

Getting Connected ●

How much time do you spend each day on Facebook? It's so easy to get caught up in the pictures and posts that seem to indicate others live better or more exciting lives than you do. Do you catch yourself wishing you could live in someone else's world? If you could go where they go, do what they do, hang out with their friends...wouldn't life be perfect? Comparing your life to someone else's can rob you of joy and gratefulness.

God created you for specific purposes, and He has a specific plan for your life. In fact, Jeremiah 29:11 reminds you, "'I know the plans I have for you,' declares the LORD, 'plans to prosper you and not to harm you, plans to give you hope and a future.'" Where you live, how you look, how much money your parents make, or what brands of clothes you wear will not bring you joy. True joy comes when you have an attitude of thankfulness. Then you can be like the apostle Paul who wrote, "I have learned to be content whatever the circumstances" (Philippians 4:11).

Today's App: Consider creating a gratitude journal. Each day write down 10 things you are grateful for. At the end of the week, recall God's goodness in your life and how He has blessed you. Why not post your praise online?

Radical Grace

Megan: "I know we are supposed to reach out to others, but this new girl is weird. I don't think she goes to church and I heard she is boy crazy. I shouldn't hang out with someone like that, right?"

God's Text: "Do not judge, or you too will be judged. For in the same way you judge others, you will be judged, and with the measure you use, it will be measured to you" (Matthew 7:1-2).

Getting Connected

When you judge others, the Bible teaches that you are condemning yourself. The truth of God's Word exposes your heart: "All have sinned and fall short of the glory of God" (Romans 3:23). Praise God you are forgiven and justified by Christ! Ask Him to help you see each person as He does—with love and grace. The new girl, a friend who made a mistake, a teacher who let you down, the boy who disappoints you, the stranger who is rude—the hurts go on and on…and so do the opportunities to extend God's grace.

You rarely know another person's full story, including what her heart is dealing with. God knows her story *and* yours. He can use you in mighty ways to love and minister to other people if you make yourself available. Ask the Lord today to help you focus on serving Him by loving others and resisting the temptation to judge. Thank Him that He is your righteous judge and that He is true to His Word.

Today's App: Think about God's message to you in John 8:7: "When they kept on questioning him, [Jesus] straightened up and said to them, 'Let any one of you who is without sin be the first to throw a stone at her.'" The only reasonable response to this challenge is to confess your sin and thank Jesus for His grace and forgiveness! Then glorify Him by reaching out to others with His radical grace.

Forgiveness Unlimited

Maddy: "I thought I could forgive Alisha, but every time I think about what she did I get even madder."

God's Text: "Peter came to Jesus and asked, 'Lord, how many times shall I forgive my brother or sister who sins against me? Up to seven times?' Jesus answered, 'I tell you, not seven times, but seventy-seven times'" (Matthew 18:21-22).

Getting Connected

Forgiveness can be a funny thing. Do you ever find yourself believing in your mind and heart, "I forgive," but then your mind flashes back to what the person did to cause you pain and you get mad all over again? How come you keep playing the offense over and over? That's a tough question. God's Word has specific instructions when it comes to how you should forgive. In Matthew 18, the disciples are asking Jesus how many times people need to forgive someone. Jesus said "seventy-seven times." Essentially what He is saying is that you need to keep on forgiving—over and over if necessary.

Jesus wants you to forgive someone when she hurts you *and* forgive her every time you remember the situation. He is teaching you how to forgive in your heart *and* in your head.

Today's App: Do you get angry when you think about how someone hurt you? Ask the Lord to help you forgive again and again. When your mind remembers the past hurt, don't count—just forgive!

Don't Stand By, Stand Up

Kamber: "I am so mad at the way she treats everyone. I just want to punch her in the face!"

God's Text: "'If your enemy is hungry, feed him; if he is thirsty, give him something to drink. In doing this, you will heap burning coals on his head.' Do not be overcome by evil, but overcome evil with good" (Romans 12:20-21). *What does this mean? Give examples)*

Getting Connected •

Bullying is in the news a lot lately. Sadly, there is always a deeper meaning behind why girls and boys bully. They are generally depressed or angry about something going on in their lives. This does not give anyone permission to harass others, however. Bullying must be taken seriously. If you feel threatened by a bully or you know someone who is feeling that way, let an adult know. With girls, bullying is usually a verbal attack of some kind, face-to-face, through texting, e-mail, or social network sites. If you *stand up* to the bully instead of fighting back, she is more likely to change her behavior. *How can you intervene? E-mail scripture*

What do we mean by "stand up"? A bully wants a dramatic response to her actions. Simply telling her she needs to stop being mean and then walking away may have a surprising effect—if not immediately, then possibly over time. When someone is bullying you, surround yourselves with friends who love and support you.

Even if the bully doesn't change, your attitude toward her can. Praying for the girl is the first step. Jesus said, "You have heard that it was said, 'Love your neighbor and hate your enemy.' But I tell you, love your enemies and pray for those who persecute you" (Matthew 5:43-44). Praying for bullies acknowledges they are people in need of God's love and grace. When you pray for them, you can't help but see them in a new light.

Today's App: Who is someone you can pray for today? Ask God to reveal to you a way you can show her God's love. Who knows, your Christlike example may just bring her closer to God. *People need love the most when they deserve it the least.*

Texting Bait

Chantal: "This guy has been flirting with me through texting. At first I thought it was sweet, but now the messages are getting suggestive. What should I do?"

God's Text: "Let no one deceive you with empty words, for because of such things God's wrath comes on those who are disobedient. Therefore do not be partners with them" (Ephesians 5:6-7).

Getting Connected

Do you get a rush of adrenaline when you hear that familiar sound—the moment your phone signals there's a text message waiting for your eyes only? Texting can be instant, fun, and personal. With the push of a button, a guy now has instant access to flirt with you. So how do you know if a message is just for fun or if it's bait to get you hooked into a bad situation? It may start innocently. A guy sends an open-ended message to see how you will respond. It can be little texts like "been thinking about you all day" or "Do u miss me?"

Some texts are intended to get a strong emotion from you, such as "luv u." The danger of taking the bait is that you end up desiring more from the relationship. That can lead to sending and receiving messages that are inappropriate. God's text today has a strong warning about being deceived by someone with empty words, and that can include text messages. Look again at the last line in Ephesians 5:7: "Therefore do not be partners with them."

The next time a text of "empty words" or inappropriateness pops up on your phone or anywhere else, delete the message *before* it hooks your heart.

Today's App: The best text message you can ever receive is from God. He has texted you through His book, the Bible. He is waiting for your reply!

Influencing Others

Sadie: "How can I be a positive influence to my friends?"

God's Text: "Esther won the favor of everyone who saw her" (Esther 2:15).

"I urge you to live a life worthy of the calling you have received. Be completely humble and gentle; be patient" (Ephesians 4:1-2).

Getting Connected

Being a godly influence in the midst of this crazy world can seem impossible. When you think of influential women in the world today, Oprah Winfrey, Michelle Obama, Hillary Clinton, Taylor Swift, Selena Gomez, and Miley Cyrus might come to mind. But have you thought about what you can learn from the influential women in the Bible?

Esther was a teenager when she was taken from her home and put into one of the biggest beauty pageants in history. After a year of beauty treatments, the king would choose one young woman out of hundreds to be his new queen. He chose Esther! There are three wonderful attributes we can learn from her about influencing others.

First, external beauty is nice, but a beautiful heart can change lives. Today's message from God's Word says that "Esther won the favor of everyone who saw her." "Favor" is defined as "the state of being approved or held in high regard." Her demeanor and personality were so pleasing she even won over the other young women being considered by the king.

Second, being willing to pray and asking others to join in encourages people to look to God for answers. When Esther was asked to risk her life and go before the king to save her people, the first thing she did was decide to pray and fast for three days and ask others to do the same. Her prayer life influenced others to be diligent in prayer.

Third, she was bold. After three days of prayer and fasting, Esther went to the king to intercede for the Jews. Going before the king without being summoned by him was punishable by death. She went anyway, knowing that if she didn't the Jews would be murdered.

When you follow Esther's model of influence, God can do amazing things through you.

Today's App: Read the short book of Esther. Start an Esther reading group with a friend or two. You'll enjoy discussing her story! Focus on Esther's attributes that made her so influential. Ask God to develop those characteristics in you.

Body Parts

Diana: "What is my role in church?"

God's Text: "Just as a body, though one, has many parts, but all its many parts form one body, so it is with Christ...If the whole body were an eye, where would the sense of hearing be? If the whole body were an ear, where would the sense of smell be? But in fact God has placed the parts in the body, every one of them, just as he wanted them to be. If they were all one part, where would the body be? As it is, there are many parts, but one body" (1 Corinthians 12:12,17-20).

Getting Connected

When Sundays roll around, do you dread waking up so you wait until your parents have to drag you out of bed? Do you fight tooth and nail to stay home instead of going to church? When you get to church, do you sit like a bump on a log, counting down the minutes until the service is over? Sundays are meant to be a time of rejuvenation, a time to recharge and prepare to live for God in the coming week. Church isn't just for your mom and dad and the older folks who are there every Sunday. Church is for you too.

In a church body, every part works together. The church needs parents and grandparents. It needs babies in the nursery, children in Sunday school, and teens in youth group. The church also needs you to be engaged and active in its mission of sharing the gospel of Jesus Christ. Read God's text message again. Every part of the body plays an integral role—including you!

Today's App: Do you go to church on autopilot? This Sunday, walk through those doors ready to hear from God, to worship Him through prayers and songs, and to actively participate in the mission of the church. Show up for God so you can step into *your* essential, unique role in the body of believers.

The Home Front

Darcy: "I only hear about missions that involve leaving the country and going to some faraway place. Isn't there anything I can do here?"

God's Text: "How, then, can they call on the one they have not believed in? And how can they believe in the one of whom they have not heard? And how can they hear without someone preaching to them?" (Romans 10:14).

Getting Connected

When you hear the word "missions," do you immediately think of going to China, Africa, or some far-off country with a name you can't pronounce? It's time to view mission work as doing the work of God *everywhere,* including right where you are living, going to school, working, and ordering your favorite iced tea. Your home turf can be as big a mission field as any faraway country. Look around. Are there lost people living next door, sitting in English class, or even in your home waiting to hear what you know about God?

When soldiers go off to war, they leave their families back home to hold down the fort, to keep up the home front. They faithfully keep life going at home. Just like soldiers, missionaries are often called to go to faraway countries, leaving others behind to take care of things. God may be calling you to keep up the home front and be a missionary in your hometown. As a Christian, it's important to realize that everywhere you go, your responsibility is to demonstrate and share the love of Christ. God has placed you in your very own mission field. All you have to do is start sharing!

Today's App: Ask God to give you sensitivity and a heart for the people within your mission field. Start praying for them. Ask God how you can help people who don't know Him.

What Would People Call You?

Nina: "I wonder how my friends would describe me if I weren't around."

God's Text: "Be very careful, then, how you live—not as unwise but as wise, making the most of every opportunity, because the days are evil" (Ephesians 5:15-16).

Getting Connected

How do you think your friends would describe you? Would it be positive or negative? Would they tell others about your love of Christ? Or do they even know you are a Christian? The way you live your life will set an example of a life lived for Christ or a life lived in the world.

The book of Acts outlines the first church and what believers acted like. "For a whole year Barnabas and Saul met with the church and taught great numbers of people. The disciples were called Christians first at Antioch" (Acts 11:26). Followers of Christ didn't come up with the nickname "Christians"! Local people called them that because they could see evidence of their love for Christ in the lives of the believers! They noticed how they followed their Savior.

What would your friends call you? Would they call you "Christian"? You may be the only Bible some people ever read. Make sure your life reflects Christ and His love.

Today's App: What does your life say to others? Ask God to make your life a reflection of His love and His promises. Dedicate your life to showing and telling others about God through your words and actions.

He Loves Me...He Loves Me Not

Janie: "My boyfriend has been pressuring me lately to go further physically. He says if I love him, I will prove it by having sex with him."

God's Text: "Husbands, love your wives, just as Christ loved the church and gave himself up for her to make her holy, cleansing her by the washing with water through the word, and to present her to himself as a radiant church, without stain or wrinkle or any other blemish, but holy and blameless" (Ephesians 5:25-27).

Getting Connected ●

The world's standards on sex are drastically different from God's standard. The world tells you, "Go ahead and have sex. It's not going to hurt anyone." Here's the truth: God created sex for our pleasure and procreation. He didn't create it to be a taboo subject in our families and churches, nor did He create it to be forbidden forever. He created it as a gift to the people He loves. A gift to be enjoyed in the right place at the right time between a married couple. Any boy who pressures you to have sex before marriage is thinking only of himself—not God, not you, and not your relationship with God.

God's text today talks about a husband loving his wife as Christ loves the church. In this illustration, you represent the church. Do you think God wants you to engage in an action He disapproves of? Something you'll regret? No! If Christ wouldn't want it for you, you shouldn't want it for you...and your boyfriend shouldn't want it for you either.

Today's verse also mentions presenting the church to God without stain, wrinkle, or blemish. God's desire is that you can give yourself to your future husband as a woman holy and blameless, without blemish. Even if you have feelings of love and your boyfriend declares the same, true love means wanting to remain whole and holy, following God's standards.

Today's App: "Love is patient, love is kind. It does not envy, it does not boast, it is not proud. It does not dishonor others, it is not self-seeking, it is not easily angered, it keeps no record of wrongs" (1 Corinthians 13:4-5). *True love is patient and not self-seeking. It does not focus on instant gratification.* Why not pray for your future husband? Ask God to bless him, watch over him, and help him remain pure for you.

Under the Umbrella

Stella: "I can't stand my teacher. She is crazy and treats me like a baby. I don't know why I should have to listen to her."

God's Text: "Let everyone be subject to the governing authorities, for there is no authority except that which God has established. The authorities that exist have been established by God. Consequently, whoever rebels against the authority is rebelling against what God has instituted, and those who do so will bring judgment on themselves" (Romans 13:1-2).

Getting Connected

In a rainstorm, using an umbrella will get you from point A to point B without looking like a wet mop. Because of the protection the umbrella provides, you are shielded from the damage the rain could do to your clothes—not to mention your hair. Think of obedience to God as an umbrella. When you are doing what He says, you are under His protection. You are protected from the negative consequences that would arise if you went outside of His instructions or principles.

In today's text from God, you learn that *every* authority figure, including your parents, teachers, principals, bosses, and perhaps even older siblings, is put in place by God. His command is that you be subject to their authority. By respecting authority figures, even the ones who make life hard sometimes, you are respecting and obeying God. If you are obedient, you will remain under God's umbrella of protection and stay safe.

But if an authority figure directs you to do something that doesn't measure up to God's standards, you need to talk to another adult who knows God's principles to make sure you do the right thing. But no matter what, always treat authority figures with respect.

Today's App: Is there an authority figure in your life you have a hard time obeying? Ask God to show you how to treat him or her with respect. As you honor authority figures, you are also honoring God.

Grace and Forgiveness

Abby: "I said something mean about another girl. Does that mean God doesn't love me anymore?"

God's Text: "God demonstrates his own love for us in this: While we were still sinners, Christ died for us" (Romans 5:8).

Getting Connected ●

Think about the last time you had a bad day or said the wrong thing at the wrong time. While all of us have those days, they can make us feel pretty lousy. God, in the midst of our times of sin, offers us grace and forgiveness. He is a God of mercy, and those mercies are new each and every day (Lamentations 3:22-23). He offers it even if you feel like you don't deserve it. All that stands in the way is whether you are willing to share with God your mistakes and ask Him for forgiveness.

"Grace" can be explained as God's *unmerited* favor. People don't deserve His forgiveness, but He offers it unconditionally. Even if you have a personal relationship with Jesus Christ, your Savior, there is a need every day to experience His forgiveness and grace. God's Word offers this promise: "If we confess our sins, he is faithful and just and will forgive us our sins and purify us from all unrighteousness." That's a wonderful promise you can claim right now!

Today's App: How about it? Do you need to ask God to forgive you for something you've done? Do you need to ask someone else to forgive you? Do you need to offer mercy to someone? Grace truly is amazing. Put it into practice today.

LIFE

On the outside, it all looked perfect. I was Miss America 2007, living my dream…and the dream of so many girls. I was really good at painting on my smile when I painted on my makeup in the morning. To the people around me, my life looked perfect. I seemed happy, but on the inside I was a wreck. Becoming Miss America was a blessing, but I lost sight of the gift I'd been given when I took my eyes off of God and relied on people to meet my needs. That's when the ups and downs became more frequent and the steady joy of my faith lessened.

Life *is* a roller coaster of circumstances. Believe me, there are going to be some huge ups and some huge downs. The only constant in life is God. Through good times and bad times, He never leaves you. He is always available to guide you if you let Him.

Love,
Lauren

More Than Kissing

Natalie: "Brian and I have kissed, but lately he's been talking about going further."

God's Text: "It is God's will that you should be sanctified: that you should avoid sexual immorality; that each of you should learn to control your own body in a way that is holy and honorable, not in passionate lust like the pagans, who do not know God" (1 Thessalonians 4:3-5).

Getting Connected

Tonight you have plans to go to the movie with your boyfriend. You've kissed before, but lately he's been talking about going further physically. What do you do? How will you handle it? The most important thing you can do is *set your boundaries before the date.* God has a very high standard when it comes to sexual purity, and you need to be firm in your commitment and establish guidelines prior to being in awkward situations. Share your boundaries early in your dating history so there will be no surprises. And if your boyfriend doesn't share your standards, which are the same as God's standards, leave him behind and find the guy God has for you.

Today's App: Consider God's standards for purity and commit to establishing physical boundaries now. Yes, even if you aren't currently dating someone. Ask God to keep you strong and to provide you with boyfriends who love and respect His standards.

When Will My Season Change?

Terri: "Life is so not fair. I'm tired of waiting for things to improve. When will my situation turn around?"

God's Text: "There is a time for everything, and a season for every activity under the heavens" (Ecclesiastes 3:1).

Getting Connected ●

On the surface, trees and plants in winter may appear dead, but underground the roots are active and growing. In the same way, we all experience seasons in life when everything seems hopeless on the surface. Our personal winters may seem dreary, but nothing could be further from the truth. Tremendous growth occurs in the winter. We can't see it because everything is happening on a deep level.

Dormancy is often the time when God prepares plants and the ground for growth. Spring is on its way. To be able to support the new growth, our roots in God need to go down deep. Allow the winter seasons—the challenges and sad times—to prepare you for the spring. Something beautiful is about to bloom!

Today's App: When things look hopeless, refuse to dwell on the immediate circumstances. Instead, ask God to give you a glimpse of what He is accomplishing in your life through your situation. Then dig your roots in Him down deep. You will need strong faith to support the growth He is going to bring forth.

God Is with You

Deborah: "I feel so alone. I don't have any friends, much less a boyfriend."

God's Text: "Be strong and courageous. Do not be afraid; do not be discouraged, for the LORD your God will be with you wherever you go" (Joshua 1:9).

Getting Connected

Sure, it would be nice to have a million friends, a cute boyfriend, and be popular at school. That sounds and looks so good, doesn't it? Relationships with other people are important, but what happens when you don't have them? Do you look to the Lord for His companionship and friendship? The one friend who will *always be with you* is Christ. He sees everything you do. He loves you. He protects you.

Who is the most powerful and influential person you can think of? Whether it's the president of the United States or the cutest actor, there is someone even more important who is with you all the time. The Creator of the universe desires a personal relationship with you! He wants to hear about every detail of your life.

Today's App: Talk to God throughout your day. When you are feeling lonely or your friends don't seem to understand where you're at, share your thoughts and secrets with the One who gave His life for you. You can also ask God to bring you a close, godly friend who will encourage your faith and joy in the Lord.

Never, Ever Quit

Olivia: "I feel like giving up. I just can't take it anymore."

God's Text: "Do you not know that in a race all the runners run, but only one gets the prize? Run in such a way as to get the prize" (1 Corinthians 9:24).

Getting Connected

Every day you have decisions to make. There are simple choices, such as what to wear or what to eat for breakfast. But sometimes as the day develops the decisions get harder. How do you respond when someone makes fun of you? Do you abandon ship when drama from girlfriends surrounds you? Sometimes it's easy to want to give up or quit. Do you think it might be easier to just stay on the ground when you've been knocked down? Getting up gets harder the more times someone delivers a blow to your ego or emotional state.

Never give up! If a runner decides to quit the race, there's absolutely no chance of winning. Stay in the race and don't let the troubles of the day defeat you. Put on your running shoes and keep going even when defeat looms.

Today's App: Think back to a past experience where you felt defeated. How did you respond? Did you let it get you down? Did you stay in the race? Determine today to run your race even when decisions get tough. Focus on meeting the needs of someone else to avoid being absorbed by your troubles. Run like the winner you are!

Physically Fit

Ava: "I don't like the way my body looks."

God's Text: "Do you not know that your bodies are temples of the Holy Spirit, who is in you, whom you have received from God? You are not your own; you were bought at a price. Therefore honor God with your bodies" (1 Corinthians 6:19-20).

Getting Connected

Life fitness can be divided into three areas: body, mind, spirit. How important is your body? God gave it to you. He created you, and He expects you to take responsibility for maintaining your physical well-being.

Do you have a pet? If so, you know there are many physical needs that need to be met. Your pet must eat, exercise, and be groomed to stay healthy. You too have physical needs that need to be met and kept in balance. Good hygiene is important in maintaining your body, as well as regular exercise and healthy food. Your body also needs rest and time to relax.

How are you doing in these areas? Do you need to make some adjustments in your habits to properly maintain the wonderful, complex body God gave you? Taking care of your physical needs will also help you maintain a positive body image.

Today's App: Evaluate how you are taking care of your body. Are you exercising regularly? Are you eating enough fruits and vegetables? Choose a new, healthy habit to start today, such as walking further or choosing an apple over a cupcake. And don't forget to thank God for your incredible body!

Gossip or Gotcha?

Isabella: "I'm so mad at one of my friends. What do I do?"

God's Text: "Without wood a fire goes out; without a gossip a quarrel dies down" (Proverbs 26:20).

Getting Connected

Have you ever been so angry toward someone that you wanted to get her back? Or maybe you've been hurt by a friend who said something about you that was false, hurtful, or just plain mean. The desire to pick up your cell phone, call your friends, and trash the other girl can be so tempting. You want to say, "Gotcha back!"

When someone hurts you, you don't have the right to hurt them back. Even though it can be more difficult, God says to stop, forgive the hurt, and let it go. And if you don't like bad things said about you, don't say bad things about others, even if you believe the words are true or deserved. God says the best way to stop gossip is simple—don't get involved.

Today's App: Have you gossiped about someone because you felt she deserved it? What do you think God would say if you said those things to Him?

Purity in Texts

Melissa: "It was only a text message. It wasn't a big deal."

God's Text: "Don't let anyone look down on you because you are young, but set an example for the believers in speech, in conduct, in love, in faith and in purity" (1 Timothy 4:12).

Getting Connected ●

You know you shouldn't say bad things about others, and maybe you are good at holding your tongue before you say something mean, damaging, or hateful. But what about writing bad things about others? Do you keep your lips tight but then let loose when your fingers are flying over the text pad? Have you sent a text message you wouldn't want your mom, your dad, or a fellow classmate to read? It's so easy to type in a few words, press a button, and voila!...a "harmless" text message is sent. Yet God sees all—even your texts.

If you don't want God to see what you send, maybe you shouldn't write the text to begin with.

Today's App: Are you texting messages you shouldn't? Would you change how or what you text if you knew God was reading it? What about your parents? Or the person referenced in your text? Think about these things the next time you let your fingers do the talking.

Glass Half Full?

Ava: "I can't get past all the bad things that have happened to me. First my parents got a divorce, then my boyfriend broke up with me, and now I am failing math. How am I supposed to get through all of this?"

God's Text: "Do not be anxious about anything, but in every situation, by prayer and petition, with thanksgiving, present your requests to God. And the peace of God, which transcends all understanding, will guard your hearts and your minds in Christ Jesus" (Philippians 4:6-7).

Getting Connected

Sometimes life is just rough. We face struggles with our families, dramas with our friends, and stresses at school that make for a crazy life. The truth is that no one's life is perfect. The question is, how are you going to handle strife when it comes knocking on your door? When you come face-to-face with obstacles, you have a choice in how to respond.

God tells us that He has given us peace. Jesus said, "Peace I leave with you; my peace I give you. I do not give to you as the world gives. Do not let your hearts be troubled and do not be afraid" (John 14:27). God has freely given us His grace, and with that special gift His peace flows into our lives. Christ's peace is the refusal to define life by the worst that has happened to you. Choosing Christ's peace lets you define your life by the things He has blessed you with.

Today's App: Even though today might be bogged down with troubles, what blessing has God given you to focus on instead? Choose to put the bad things in life on the back burner and make God's blessings your focus.

From Mess to Masterpiece

Claire: "Can God take my sins and make something good out of them? I feel like there is no hope for me."

God's Text: "None of the offenses they have committed will be remembered against them. Because of the righteous things they have done, they will live" (Ezekiel 18:22).

Getting Connected

Need a little good news today? Well, you've come to the right place. God can take all of your mess—all of your sins—and make something beautiful out of it. We all mess up. Bathsheba is a perfect example of God's handiwork. Bathsheba was caught in a scandal that included adultery, murder, tragedy, and great loss. Sounds a lot like a Hollywood movie, right? Even though Bathsheba was tangled up in a web of sin, God brought her through it and even made her the mother of King Solomon...and part of the bloodline of our Savior, Jesus Christ!

The moral of the story is that God can take all of your mess and not only clean it up but make something gorgeous out of it. If you tell God about your mistakes and give them over to His grace, He will work in your life. And girl, God does amazing things! Don't let your sins, mistakes, failures, or bad judgment keep you from becoming the transformed masterpiece God is eager to create and work with.

Today's App: Be at peace knowing God will take whatever your mess is and make something beautiful out of it if you ask Him to! No matter how bad it is, and trust me, God has seen some pretty bad things, He can form a masterpiece out of your mess.

Hitting a Curveball

Avery: "I'm having a tough time with my parents' divorce. I feel like no one understands because my family used to be so close."

God's Text: "Be strong and courageous. Do not be afraid; do not be discouraged, for the Lord your God will be with you wherever you go" (Joshua 1:9).

Getting Connected •

Do you ever feel like life has thrown you a curveball? Those unexpected trials that seem overwhelming? Every good baseball player learns how to hit a curveball. When life throws you one, God can use it to shape you into the person He longs for you to be.

God is writing your story, and trials are just chapters in the big book of your life. Out of the pain, God can strengthen you. Whether you are dealing with the divorce of your parents, the death of a loved one, or even just mustering up the nerve to try out for a part in the school play, remember God is *always* with you. He is the one constant in your life who will never let you down.

If you are facing something difficult right now, take a moment to write down what scares you. Then lift it to God and place your fear in His hands.

Today's App: Talk to God. Tell Him you are desperate for His help and don't feel capable of letting go without His help. Ask Him to show you how you can view this situation in your life as a positive.

The Blessing of Convictions

Cora: "Mariah wanted me to go to a party where I knew they were drinking. I didn't feel right about it, but she really pressured me. I gave in and now I feel awful."

God's Text: "When [the Holy Spirit] comes, he will prove the world to be in the wrong about sin and righteousness and judgment" (John 16:8).

Getting Connected

It's easy to get pulled into situations where your convictions can be compromised. Your heart wants to do what's right, but when pressure comes from your friends your head says it's okay to "cave in" to justify your actions. Later, when you're alone, do you ever feel guilt or remorse?

As a believer, God gave you the Holy Spirit to show you the difference between right and wrong. When you face a compromising situation ask these questions: Does this action go against God's Word? Would my parents approve or disapprove? Will this action bring me closer to the Lord or pull me away? Can this action damage my Christian testimony to unbelievers? Allow the Holy Spirit to be your guide, and listen for His voice inside you.

Conviction may seem like a curse sometimes, but truly it is a blessing. If you follow the prompting of the Holy Spirit, you will be spared a lot of heartache and regret. While people may give you grief temporarily, remind yourself that you are pursuing *God's best* for your life.

Today's App: Here's a helpful prayer:

Heavenly Father, please help me know for sure when the Holy Spirit is prompting me. I want my heart to be sensitive to Your will for my life. Give me the courage to stand up for what You are showing me is right and realize You are in complete control of my life. In Jesus' name. Amen.

A Way Out

Kayla: "I face the same temptations all the time. I'm not sure how long I can keep resisting."

God's Text: "No temptation has overtaken you except what is common to mankind. And God is faithful; he will not let you be tempted beyond what you can bear. But when you are tempted, he will also provide a way out so that you can endure it" (1 Corinthians 10:13).

Getting Connected

You know that God forgives, but something may be wrong when you keep asking Him to forgive Sin #50 over and over again. Temptation is right in front of your eyes, and your mind is trying to justify why it won't be as bad this time around: "Remember, you can always ask for forgiveness later."

How do you fight temptation and the desire to compromise? First, know your convictions *before* the temptation happens. Decide how you will respond when the sticky situation arises. Second, if you're facing temptation, remember today's text message. God *always provides* a way of escape. For example, if you are tempted to go further with your boyfriend physically than you know you should, be realistic. Tell your boyfriend you will not compromise in this area. Set a boundary to help you honor God, such as deciding to avoid the two of you being alone in a room together.

Finally, pray for wisdom. Stand firm and God will honor you for following His standards!

Today's App: Talk to God about facing temptations:

Lord, help me figure out how to deal with temptations before they come. Show me the right path. Give me the courage to say no, and help me set good boundaries. Let others see Your light in me. In Your name. Amen.

Monkey Business

Tracy: "My biology teacher believes in evolution. Is it true we came from monkeys?"

God's Text: "God made the wild animals according to their kinds, the livestock according to their kinds, and all the creatures that move along the ground according to their kinds. And God saw that it was good. Then God said, 'Let us make mankind in our image, in our likeness, so that they may rule over the fish in the sea and the birds in the sky, over the livestock and all the wild animals, and over all the creatures that move along the ground'" (Genesis 1:25-26).

Getting Connected

Evolution is a tough issue, but it's one you may face for years. First, remind yourself the Bible is true—every bit of it. That also means it is trustworthy. So when you're faced with evolution theory, start with the beginning of God's Word—the book of Genesis. In the first chapter, there is a distinct difference in the creation of animals and the creation of man. Animals were created by God's word. He spoke the creation of the world and animals into existence. But man was created in the image of God.

God's Word is clear that man did not evolve from another created creature. While animals may have evolved within their own species, there is no scientific evidence that mankind evolved from animals. Only humans have souls—an eternal soul that makes a personal relationship with their Creator possible (Genesis 2:7). You are uniquely created to be in relationship with God. Believe His truth. Anything else is just monkey business.

Today's App: Still confused and want more answers? Study this topic further. Ask friends, parents, or a youth pastor to help you explore Creationism in more depth. You want to have the confidence of God's answers firmly planted in your heart and mind.

Holding Hostages

Karsyn: "I feel like church and youth group are the 'God' part of my life. School and weekends are more about friends and fun. Isn't that normal?"

God's Text: "You shall have no other gods before me" (Exodus 20:3).

Getting Connected

When you examine your daily life, is God in first place? Or do other things or people get in the way? These other pursuits might be things you forget God can see. Maybe you've separated them from the "God part" so you can be in control and not "bother" God with the "little decisions" you make.

The Lord desires all of your strengths, gifts, and even your weakness and flaws. So when you keep even a few of these away from Him, you open yourself to the world and more opportunities for sin to enter your life. You might become captive to sin instead of strengthening your connection with God. The Lord tells us He came to set the captives free and release the prisoners from darkness (Isaiah 61:1). What do you need to be freed from today? Give it to God and ask Him to take care of it.

Today's App: Trust God enough to give Him all areas of your life—even the ones you've been holding back. "Do not conform to the pattern of this world, but be transformed by the renewing of your mind. Then you will be able to test and approve what God's will is—his good, pleasing and perfect will" (Romans 12:2). You'll be glad you did!

Rejection Reality

Shawna: "There is a group of girls at my school I really want to hang out with. I feel like they don't want me and that really hurts. What's wrong with me? Why would they reject me?"

God's Text: "You are a chosen people, a royal priesthood, a holy nation, God's special possession, that you may declare the praises of him who called you out of darkness into his wonderful light" (1 Peter 2:9).

Getting Connected

Rejection. We all deal with it at one time or another. It can leave us feeling insecure and alone. God's Word says, "For the sake of his great name the LORD will not reject his people, because the LORD was pleased to make you his own" (1 Samuel 12:22). *God chose you* because He delights in you. He accepts you, not out of pity, but because He crafted you and longs to be in relationship with you. You weren't meant to barely get by in life. You were meant to experience abundance and joy and a harvest of great things!

You are far from rejected. There is nothing wrong with you. God knows all about you and He loves you. The Lord tells us He absolutely will never forget you. In fact, He has you engraved (tattooed) on the palms of His hands (Isaiah 49:15-16). Think about it! Your name is engraved on the hands of the Almighty! Rejection on earth is tiny in comparison to the acceptance of your Lord, who holds even the oceans in His hands.

Today's App: Ask the Lord to help you wrap your arms around the truths from His Word shared today. Let Him use all things in your life to establish a deeper relationship with Him.

Pressing Pressures

Kris: "I feel so overwhelmed. How can I get rid of some of this pressure?"

God's Text: "Do not be anxious about anything, but in every situation, by prayer and petition, with thanksgiving, present your requests to God. And the peace of God, which transcends all understanding, will guard your hearts and your minds in Christ Jesus" (Philippians 4:6-7).

Getting Connected •

Do you often feel overwhelmed? Do you feel pressure bearing down on you from all directions? Stress can build as you process the expectations of parents, the demands of schoolwork, and the worries that whiz through your mind. And that's not even mentioning the drama in relationships with friends. So, what can you do?

First, take the time to pray! Ask the Lord for peace in your heart. Second, go before the Lord with a thankful heart. He wants to hear all your requests, down to the last detail, but He also wants you to recognize His faithfulness and His blessings in your life. The result will be a peace that will calm your anxious heart.

Today's App: Do you consider yourself someone who has a hard time handling the pressures of life? Are you taking your troubles and cares to the Lord through prayer? Claim the promise of today's verses, Philippians 4:6-7, and rest in the peace of God.

The Picture You Are Posting

Savannah: "My friends post the most ridiculous status remarks and pictures on Facebook. It's so embarrassing when they have tagged me in pictures I know my church friends would disapprove of."

God's Text: "[The LORD] has shown you, O mortal, what is good. And what does the LORD require of you? To act justly and to love mercy and to walk humbly with your God" (Micah 6:8).

Getting Connected

Your witness can speak volumes in social media circles. Every time you post something on Facebook, Twitter, a blog, and other media, it is something that *cannot* be taken back. Even if you delete something you regret posting, it remains out there forever.

We *encourage* you to carefully consider what you do, what you post, and even what you read and look at on other people's pages. Facebook can be a great way to connect with friends and keep up with everyone. God's Word includes instructions you can use socially. Paul wrote, "Nor should there be obscenity, foolish talk or coarse joking, which are out of place, but rather thanksgiving" (Ephesians 5:4). Do the comments you are about to post encourage others or hurt someone? Do they reflect your faith or cause others to question your faith? Are your activities with your friends uplifting and honoring to God? Are the pictures and texts being posted things you'd be comfortable having your parents and youth pastor read? When activities are questionable, leave the situation so you don't get caught in compromising situations. When in doubt while posting, hit delete instead of send!

Use these media outlets to express your development in Christ. If you are always posting statuses about being mad or angry at someone, you can see how that might cause people to think Christians are judgmental and angry all the time. And remember, what you post online in some ways becomes your identity to the world. Show your lasting love for God instead of highlighting temporary emotions.

Today's App: Ask God if there's anything on your public pages that needs to be deleted. Remember: When in doubt, hit delete. Set an example for your friends by becoming more careful about what you post. It will be good for others, and it will benefit you as well.

A Lonely Heart

Ella: "I feel so alone. My boyfriend broke up with me, my best friend moved away, and I don't like talking to my parents. I want my old life back."

God's Text: "Do not fear, for I am with you; do not be dismayed, for I am your God. I will strengthen you and help you; I will uphold you with my righteous right hand" (Isaiah 41:10).

Getting Connected ●

Have you experienced a season of loneliness? Junior high and high school can be challenging, emotional times for girls. You may find yourself unsure of who to trust or rely on as you figure out life. This uncertainty can leave you feeling incredibly lonely.

How can you handle loneliness? First, don't feel sorry for yourself. Instead, look at this time as an opportunity to grow in your prayer life. Why not pray for better friends, stronger friends, and for you to become a better friend? People were created to be in community. God knows where you are and what you're experiencing. Have you asked Him what He wants you to learn in this season of loneliness?

Keep your head up and trust that God has something good for you to discover during this time in your walk with Him.

Today's App: If you are feeling alone and lonely, remember that God is right there with you. Ask the Lord to show you someone you can reach out to today. Keep in mind that if you want a friend, you have to be a friend.

Just for Now?

McKenna: "I'm having trouble making decisions. What's wrong with me?"

God's Text: "Get wisdom, get understanding; do not forget my words or turn away from them" (Proverbs 4:5).

Getting Connected ●

Decisions...decisions at every turn! Who to hang out with. Where to apply for a job. Should you try out for a sport this year. Which shoes to buy. Here's a good truth to keep in mind: When you make day-to-day choices, they are usually not permanent. If you're struggling in a friendship, perhaps you need to take a little break from that person. You may need to find part-time work to help pay for something that is important to you right now. You may like tennis this year, but not next year. So don't stress out too much when faced with decisions that need to be made. Feel the freedom of walking in faith and making those daily choices with ease because they are not forever, but instead are "just for now."

There are some choices that involve lasting blessings or consequences. You can lean on God for wisdom and understanding when those decisions arise. The psalmist wrote, "Show me your ways, LORD, teach me your paths" (Psalm 25:4). How do you get wisdom? There are four things you can do to make sure you are on the right track: 1) Follow God's directions, 2) always pray about each choice before you make it, 3) get advice from someone you trust, such as your mom or dad, and 4) look at your motives and the possible outcomes. Every decision you make has the potential for positive or negative consequences. If you follow these basic principles, everyone wins! You will be making godly decisions. Those are the kind that are the best for you!

Today's App: Have you been trying to make a decision on something but haven't done it yet? Make sure you are on the right track by looking at the four steps to decision making. Write them down...and put them where you will see them daily. This is one decision you'll be glad you made.

Deny...Deny...Deny

Cassie: "I'm so scared to be myself around my friends. I am doing and saying things I never dreamed would be part of my life so I'll fit in. I feel trapped! Can you help?"

God's Text: "Now faith is confidence in what we hope for and assurance about what we do not see" (Hebrews 11:1).

Getting Connected

The enemy—the devil—would love for you to think that the Word of God is a lie, that it doesn't help, that it doesn't have power, and that it can't change your life. Remember what happened to Eve? The serpent got Eve to doubt God and then deny what God had told her. She and Adam ate fruit from the tree of the knowledge of good and evil, which God had specifically told them not to do. This "original sin" separated the two— and all of humanity!—from intimate fellowship with God. (Praise God that Jesus came to reestablish our relationship with God!)

When you doubt and deny the truths in God's Word, you let fear in and you can block out the faith. And when you live in fear of not fitting in, it's easy to make bad choices to fit with the crowd. Maybe you've been tempted to be mean to someone, to gossip, to be physical with your boyfriend, to experiment with alcohol or drugs, or to cheat. Just like Adam and Eve, sin will separate you from intimate fellowship with God.

But you can trust God and His Word! "Those who find [wisdom] find life and receive favor from the LORD" (Proverbs 8:35). Don't be afraid to be yourself. Keep God's Word in your heart, and you will have confidence to be who you are in Christ.

Today's App: How are you doing when it comes to God's Word? Find life and truth and acceptance in the Word by memorizing Scripture one verse at a time, one week at a time. Think about it! In one year you will know 52 new verses and your lifeline to the Lord will be stronger.

When Your Plans Aren't God's

Peyton: "I know I want to do musical theater and pursue a career as an actor on Broadway. But I don't know if this is what God wants for me. I've heard He wants to give us our desires, but how can I know when my wishes are His plan for me?"

God's Text: "'I know the plans I have for you,' declares the LORD, 'plans to prosper you and not to harm you, plans to give you hope and a future'" (Jeremiah 29:11).

Getting Connected

In our busy lives we face countless new opportunities to try, groups or clubs to join, and classes to sign up for. Then we wake up one morning still tired and realize we've completely overcommitted ourselves. How can we know which desires to follow? Which choices fit with God's plans for us?

It's great to have goals, hopes, and dreams! And God most assuredly cares about what you care about because He loves you. The passions and gifts you have were given to you by Him! It's wonderful that you want to use them for His glory. Even if you're unsure of whether a choice is the best one, God will use everything you do for your good if you let Him (Romans 8:28).

The danger creeps in when you shut down the voice of God. If you allow your passions to distract you from spending alone time with God, you may be more susceptible to justifying your desires instead of really wanting His input. You also may have a harder time discerning between what is right or wrong.

Today's App: Have you been spending enough time with the Lord? If you're confused about your passions and what choices you should or should not make, clear up some time to sit with your heavenly Father. Ask Him for advice and wisdom. Write out your dreams and pray over them . Remember, God loves you!

Chain Reaction

Aubrey: "That girl accused me of lying! I was so mad I yelled at her."

God's Text: "The tongue is a small part of the body, but it makes great boasts. Consider what a great forest is set on fire by a small spark" (James 3:5).

Getting Connected

Talk about a "drama girl"! You know, the person who lets a 50-cent event get a 500-dollar reaction. Going off on someone when you're hurt or falsely accused might be your natural response. However, if you follow that gut response, you risk becoming a "hurler," someone who spews from the mouth...and it seems like the not-so-godly words always come out the loudest. God compares the tongue to a small spark that can start a forest fire. That means your words can get you into a lot of trouble!

Jesus gives us a perfect example of the correct reaction for tough situations. As He was brought before Pontius Pilate and the Jewish priests accused Him of all sorts of false sins, Jesus responded with silence. He didn't defend himself against the lies. He didn't yell or scream that they were deceivers. Pilate asked Him why He wasn't answering the charges, "but Jesus still made no reply." Jesus knew the truth of who He was and what He did. Therefore He didn't acknowledge the false accusations of wrongdoing. Maybe the next time you are confronted with a situation where you have been wronged, you can stop before you react, ask God to give you wisdom, and respond more like Jesus did.

Today's App: Ask God to help you think before you speak and to make your reactions more like those of Jesus. Seek clarity and peace of mind in times when there are lies, chaos, and deceivers around you. Sometimes silence is the most profound, godly response there is.

Think on This

Ashley: "Nothing good ever happens to me. Every time I try to do something right, something happens to mess up my plans. I'm an epic failure."

God's Text: "As he thinks within himself, so he is" (Proverbs 23:7 NASB).

Getting Connected

God has a good future planned for you, but Satan is out to destroy it. He'll do anything to prevent you from living God's plan. Thoughts of insignificance and unworthiness are one of Satan's tools to trap you in a state of despair. He makes them seem so real by disguising them with partial truths. These unhealthy images are his lures to destroy you—but you don't have to take the bait.

Your thoughts influence who you think you are and what you do. When you struggle with feelings of failure, it's usually because your thoughts have veered off course. That's when it's time to change direction! Shift your mind to healthy thoughts and you'll begin to feel better about yourself. Focusing on the positive will fill you with hope and confidence for the future. Why? Because feelings follow thoughts. Really!

Have you heard the expression "You are what you eat"? In regard to your spiritual health, you are also what you think! Do you want to change your feelings? Change your thoughts.

Today's App: Write down how you're feeling. Are you anxious, depressed, lonely, afraid, angry? Ask God to help you identify the thoughts that are influencing your negative feelings. Then ask Him to help you replace those thoughts with healthy thoughts. Write some of those thoughts down and say them out loud. It may feel awkward at first, but do it anyway. Refuse to meditate on the lies Satan throws at you. Declare the truth until you feel it and believe it!

GPS for Your Life

Riley: "I have no idea what to do!"

God's Text: "I will instruct you and teach you in the way you should go; I will counsel you with my loving eye on you" (Psalm 32:8).

Getting Connected ●

Have you heard of an activity called Geo-caching? It's where a person uses a handheld GPS device and goes on a hi-tech scavenger hunt. Oftentimes, the participant finds GPS directions posted online and then uses her own device to get there. The game can take people down city streets, through parks, and on walking trails. Once the geo-cacher gets to the end of the directions, there's typically a "cache"—a hidden prize.

The Bible is God's GPS device for you. He filled it with directions to lead you to the treasure of faith, divine wisdom, and life purpose. Just like using your GPS app, you would get lost on your spiritual journey without God's Word. As a Christ follower, you also have a three-letter pathfinder: G-O-D. Are you letting Him guide your way?

Today's App: Are you confused about which direction to take? God's Word is your accurate GPS for life's journey. Trust Him to advise you and watch over you. He will lead you on the best paths.

Death Is the Destiny

Alexia: "My friend's mom just died of cancer. Everyone is really sad. I'm not sure what to do or say."

God's Text: "To me, to live is Christ and to die is gain" (Philippians 1:21).

Getting Connected ●

Death is a fact of life. It's okay to be sad. It's okay to cry. Jesus wept for His friend Lazarus when he died. Grieving just means you miss the person. "Precious in the sight of the LORD is the death of his faithful servants" (Psalm 116:15). God cherishes His faithful servants, and He doesn't forget them.

Being with God is what we were created for. When believers in Christ die, they enter into God's presence! So let yourself grieve, but don't get lost in it. Don't become overwhelmed by the thought of death. God has a wonderful plan for His children—and that includes you!

What can you do when someone experiences loss? Being a good friend requires a very rare quality—being a good listener. You can't fix the sadness for your friend, but you can be there for her. Sitting with her, letting her share her thoughts...or maybe just sitting quietly to show your support. Write her a note, put together a goody bag of her favorite comforts, and let her know you are praying for her and her family. Don't avoid her because you aren't sure what to say. It may feel awkward, but your presence and faith will help ease her loss.

Today's App: If you know someone who has lost a loved one, whether recently or long ago, get your pen out and write an encouraging note. Let her know you're thinking about her.

Helping the Struggling

Ellie: "How do I love the people around me when they aren't living to please God?"

God's Text: "They exchanged the truth about God for a lie, and worshiped and served created things rather than the Creator—who is forever praised. Amen" (Romans 1:25).

Getting Connected

Everywhere you turn—school, the internet, movies, television, popular songs—there are lies and misconceptions about how to live a good life. The advice people present is colored by their values—and if they don't know God, they won't be following His principles. Their views and their lives will be tainted by sin. The Bible makes it clear how God feels about sin.

How can you guard your faith and life to stay holy and yet still show concern for those struggling with sin? First, be careful of your words. Do you make fun of people who are struggling? Do you talk about them behind their backs? That misses the mark of being Christlike. Instead, you can engage them in conversation. Find out why they have the values they do. Approach them in love without condemnation. Jesus demonstrated love. "God demonstrates his own love for us in this: While we were still sinners, Christ died for us" (Romans 5:8). Christ died for the person you want to help too. The next time you know someone is struggling, pray for her. Have a listening ear, and when you have the opportunity, gently share about Jesus and the wisdom in God's Word.

Today's App: A hot topic for teens is sex. God desires for you and your friends to remain pure. If you know someone who is struggling in this area, reach out to them with God's wisdom and through prayer:

> Lord, please help me become a compassionate person
> to my struggling friend. Give me patience and an opening
> to reveal Your love and wisdom. Give me the best words
> to share Your views on sexuality. Help my friend turn
> to You for strength. I want to demonstrate Your love so
> she'll want to know You. In Your name I pray. Amen.

Truth or Consequences

Anna Jo: "Is there really anything wrong with a little white lie?"

God's Text: "Whoever walks in integrity walks securely, but whoever takes crooked paths will be found out" (Proverbs 10:9).

Getting Connected

How many times have you altered the truth to fit your circumstances? The Bible teaches that your words should line up with His Word, which is truth. You are to become more and more like Christ. Yes, it is hard to stick to the truth when it can be painful or difficult to deal with...or when you want to avoid something. "There are six things the LORD hates, seven that are detestable to him: haughty eyes, a lying tongue, hands that shed innocent blood, a heart that devises wicked schemes, feet that are quick to rush into evil, a false witness who pours out lies and a person who stirs up conflict in the community" (Proverbs 6:16-19). Psalm 51:6 highlights the importance of following God's wisdom: "You desired faithfulness even in the womb; you taught me wisdom in that secret place."

You can ask God for wisdom so you will know His truths and practice them daily. Have you ever noticed that once a lie is told, it is easier to do it again? Or that one lie often leads to more lies? When you open the door to compromising God's principles, the end result is not pretty. Always be aware that God is present in you through the Holy Spirit. He sees and knows everything you do and say.

Today's App: Purpose today to let your "yes" be yes and your "no" be no. Stay honest and love people through the filter of God's principles. Enjoy the blessings of your personal relationship with the Creator of the universe!

Dispelling the Darkness

Makayla: "I'm depressed. Life is hard and everything feels so dark. Why do I feel so down?"

God's Text: "The LORD is close to the brokenhearted and saves those who are crushed in spirit" (Psalm 34:18).

Getting Connected ●

Do you ever feel like the walls are closing in? Does darkness overtake you spiritually and emotionally? When this happens, are the feelings temporary or do they linger for a month or more? If you are feeling down consistently, you may be experiencing depression, which can be serious. Perhaps you've endured something traumatic or the loss of someone or something special. Depression can come when life gets difficult. Talk to God about it. And talk to your parents about what's going on. Your feelings may be the result of a chemical imbalance in your body. If you can't "shake the sadness off," ask your parents to take you to a doctor for a checkup.

If the down feelings you experience come and go without sucking you into a dark pit, pray about it. Spend time in God's Word. Read from the book of Psalms. David writes about how he fought depression and sorrow. He turned to God and asked for help each time.

Today's App: Christ is the light within you. He will help you overcome the darkness. Seek Him first thing every day. Memorize His Word. When feelings of darkness are heavy, meditate on Scripture and ask the Lord to give you strength. It also helps to talk with a person you trust and respect—someone who knows and lives for Christ.

Life Preserver

Shelby: "I just got bad news. I'm really upset and feeling desperate."

God's Text: "[Jesus said,] Peace I leave with you; my peace I give you. I do not give to you as the world gives. Do not let your hearts be troubled and do not be afraid" (John 14:27).

Getting Connected

Have you ever heard of "Tornado Alley"? If you live in Oklahoma, those two words get your attention every spring. In the blink of an eye the weather can change. What started as a beautiful, calm day can quickly turn into a violent storm. Life can be like the unpredictable Oklahoma weather. In an instant, a crisis can darken and stir up your world. It might be a betrayal, a breakup, gossip, a loss, and you frantically search for help. Let God's Word be your lifeline! Today's verse on peace is great for any day, but especially on days when emotions spin out of control. Really focus on the last line: "Do not let your hearts be troubled and do not be afraid"!

Jesus is your life preserver in any storm. Put Him on, grab onto God's truth in His Word, and don't be afraid when storm clouds come your way.

Today's App: If you are entering a storm, have your lifeline ready! Ask Jesus for His help and dive into God's Word. "Then you will experience God's peace, which exceeds anything we can understand. His peace will guard your hearts and minds as you live in Christ Jesus" (Philippians 4:7 NLT).

Patience Is a Virtue

Zoe: "I've prayed and prayed and still haven't gotten an answer from God. I guess I'll take care of this myself!"

God's Text: "Since ancient times no one has heard, no ear has perceived, no eye has seen any God besides you, who acts on behalf of those who wait" (Isaiah 64:4).

Getting Connected •

If you have ever been to Disney World, you know the annoyance of waiting in line for the rides. The lines last forever and the rides go by in a flash! What do you think would happen if you decided to cut to the front of the line? You'd probably be forced to the back of the line...or maybe not even be allowed to ride at all. When it comes to God, sometimes you have to wait too. You've heard people talk about God's timing. Have you sometimes wondered when that time would come? It's so tempting to go ahead and cut in line instead of waiting to hear from God!

Abraham and Sarah prayed for years for a child, but no baby came. Instead of continuing to wait on the Lord, even after God promised Abraham a great nation would come from him, Abraham and Sarah decided to create their own plan. They essentially wanted to take cuts. Abraham and Sarah's slave Hagar conceived a child they named Ishmael. Because the child was outside of God's will and plan, God foretold the troubles Ishmael would have. When people take matters into their own hands, they alter the path God wanted them to take.

God's plan and timing are perfect—so worth the wait!

Today's App: Is there an area in your life that you're waiting on God about? Ask Him to give you patience and strength to resist the temptation of taking charge and doing it your way in your timing. God's very best is the reward for patiently waiting for His instructions and go-ahead.

Misfit

Sophie: "I want to do the right thing, but it seems like I always end up making bad choices."

God's Text: "I do not understand what I do. For what I want to do I do not do, but what I hate I do…Thanks be to God, who delivers me through Jesus Christ our Lord! So then, I myself in my mind am a slave to God's law, but in my sinful nature a slave to the law of sin" (Romans 7:15,25).

Getting Connected

Have you ever put your shoes on the wrong feet or one of your contacts in the wrong eye? It just doesn't feel quite right. In fact, it can be downright painful! It's the same when you are out of God's will. Life just doesn't feel right.

God has given you His guidelines for life in the Bible. Think of it as a "how to" for getting through each day. The principles God gives are not there to make life more difficult or less fun. They are given to help make your life more comfortable and safer.

Doing things God's way doesn't mean it will always be the easiest route, but it will go a lot smoother. When you don't do life His way, you shouldn't feel right! That's what helps you know you're on the wrong path or headed the wrong direction. "Be imitators of God, as beloved children" (Ephesians 5:1 NASB). How can you imitate God without knowing His Word? Breaking bad habits and replacing them with good ones can only be accomplished by studying the life of Jesus Christ and reading the Bible.

Today's App: Wear something in a different manner than usual for the next 24 hours. Let the strangeness remind you to follow God's ways instead of your own.

Giving In

Tory: "Okay, I feel guilty, but I just threw up so I'll be able to squeeze into my prom dress this weekend."

God's Text: "In the paths of the wicked are snares and pitfalls, but those who would preserve their life stay far from them" (Proverbs 22:5).

Getting Connected

Have you ever decided to "experiment" with sin and justify it by saying, "Just this once is no big deal"? It may work for the moment, but it puts you on a fast track to negative consequences. There's an old saying that is quite wise: "Sin will take you further than you want to go, keep you longer than you want to stay, and cost you more than you want to pay."

God's Word is clear about how sin leads you into bondage. In His text message today, you're told that the person who messes with sin will face pitfalls. We don't use "pitfall" much in conversations these days, do we? But think of an action movie where the bad guy falls into a hidden pit set up by the hero. *Crash!* And he never gets out on his own. God wants you to be healthy and to develop self-control as a fruit of the Holy Spirit living in you. When you take a step toward a pit, you'll end up empty and hurting.

Pray, giving God your body and your body image. Ask Him to show you ways that you are "fearfully and wonderfully" made (Psalm 139:14). Trust Him! Keep your focus on Him, not on temporary things.

Today's App: Whatever the temptation, step away from the pit! And if your struggle is with how you look, write down this scripture and stick it on your bathroom mirror: "I urge you, brothers and sisters, in view of God's mercy, to offer your bodies as a living sacrifice, holy and pleasing to God—this is your true and proper worship" (Romans 12:1).

On Hold

Heather: "I'm so ready to move on! All of my friends are driving, going out with their boyfriends, and doing fun stuff, but I'm sitting alone at home. When do I get to experience the world?"

God's Text: "Be still before the LORD and wait patiently for him; do not fret when people succeed in their ways, when they carry out their wicked schemes" (Psalm 37:7).

Getting Connected •

Patience is a tough characteristic to grasp and master for most people. With today's emphasis on instant gratification and speedy responses, it can be tough when you have to wait for something. What was the last thing you had to wait for?

Elijah was a prophet of God with a message for King Ahab. There would not be rain or dew until *Elijah* commanded it. Needless to say, the king was not a happy camper. He chased after Elijah to kill him. The Lord provided Elijah with a place of refuge, food, and water to sustain him. This was no Holiday Inn. Elijah stayed near the Wadi Cherith (a small brook), and ravens brought him meat to eat. First Kings 17:7 reports, "Some time later the brook dried up because there had been no rain in the land." Elijah stayed at the brook even after it dried up until God told him what to do next.

Does God have you in a holding pattern with something or someone? God has you where He wants you for a reason. Don't move without Him.

Today's App: Make a list of some things that are worth waiting for. Ask God to give you patience just as Elijah had at the Wadi. God's best is waiting for you.

Lukewarm Love

Emma: "I love God, but I don't have the time or energy to put my whole self into serving Him. There are too many other things going on right now."

God's Text: "I know your deeds, that you are neither cold nor hot. I wish you were either one or the other! So, because you are lukewarm—neither hot nor cold—I am about to spit you out of my mouth" (Revelation 3:15-16).

Getting Connected

As a new bride, one young woman would always sit in the "middle seat" of the family pickup truck. She wanted to be as close as possible to her new husband. As the years went by, the married woman no longer sat in the seat next to her husband. Instead she sat by the window. This created a person-sized space between them. One day the woman asked her husband, "How come there's a seat between us? It hasn't always been like this." The husband replied, "I'm not the one who moved away."

In your walk with the Lord, you are either moving closer to Him or further away. God wants your whole heart! He doesn't want your half-hearted devotion. Did you catch how the Lord feels about "lukewarm" believers? He wants to spit them out of His mouth! What does this mean for you? "Lukewarm" is defined as "having or showing little zeal or enthusiasm." When it comes to your life with God, are you indifferent? Do you let other things choke out your enthusiasm for doing God's work? Do you spend more time focusing on what clothes you have, who you are dating, and where you're going for vacation? When it comes to God's desire for you, He wants *all* of you!

Today's App: Which direction are you traveling today? Toward God or away from Him? Ask Him to renew your passion for Him and His guidance. And when He invites you on a journey, be sure to sit as close to Him as possible!

About Robin

Robin Marsh is an Emmy-nominated, national award-winning journalist. She's received many accolades, including excellence in feature reporting from the National Academy of Television Journalists, honors from the Society of Professional Journalists, and "Oklahoma's Journalist of the Year." The Girl Scouts honored Robin as a "Woman of Distinction." Her series on breast cancer is on display at the Museum of Broadcast Communications (Chicago).

A veteran journalist on television news for almost 30 years, Robin currently anchors the morning news on KWTV-News 9, the CBS affiliate in Oklahoma City. She served on the board of directors for the Baptist Foundation of Oklahoma and supports numerous charities.

Using her influence in broadcasting to open doors to share Jesus, Robin enjoys being a motivational speaker and sharing about Jesus Christ. She leads retreats for girls and women, and a personal highlight was sharing her testimony with 7000 students at Falls Creek Church Camp in Oklahoma.

Robin is an accomplished horsewoman who competed in rodeos and Oklahoma "play days." She and her husband, Keith, have an 11-year-old son.

About Lauren

Lauren Nelson was crowned Miss America in 2007. She received the prestigious TOYA Award, being honored as one of the "Ten Outstanding Young Americans" by the United States Junior Chamber Organization in 2008. During her tenure as Miss America, Lauren traveled the United States to promote internet safety for children. She lends her name to numerous organizations but has a special place in her heart for the Children's Miracle Network.

A graduate of the University of Central Oklahoma, Lauren holds a degree in public relations. She currently is a news anchor for KWTV-News 9, the CBS affiliate in Oklahoma City. She also speaks at numerous women's events, youth retreats, and charity functions.

An accomplished singer and performer, Lauren costarred with Shirley Jones and Patrick Cassidy in "Carousel" and sang the national anthem and other songs for several professional sporting events.

Lauren and her husband, Randy, lead worship Sunday mornings (contemporary service) and Wednesday nights for the youth at their church.

Robin and Lauren are wotking on their next book

God, Girls, & Guys!

• • •

Authentic. **Real.** *Transparent.*

Unveiled is the ministry of two passionate women.
Miss America 2007 Lauren Nelson and award-winning
television news anchor Robin Marsh team up to
reach girls with the good news of Jesus Christ.

The mission of Unveiled Ministries is to connect
young women spiritually and socially so they
can become confident women of God.

MINISTRIES

*And we all, who with unveiled faces reflect the Lord's glory,
are being transformed into his image with ever increasing
glory, which comes from the Lord, who is the Spirit.*

2 CORINTHIANS 3:18

Connect with Robin & Lauren

www.withunveiledfaces.com   *info@withunveiledfaces.com*
  Twitter: *@withunveiled*   Facebook: *withunveiledfaces*